All I Ever Wanted...

Stories of children
of the incarcerated

All I Ever Wanted...

Was her to tuck me in when I was little.

Was him to pick me up and throw me in the air.

Was her to be on the empty side when I ran into the room and jumped onto the bed because it was thundering outside.

Was him to be there at my Sweet Sixteen when it was time for the Daddy-Daughter Dance.

Was a mommy to ask what a period was, or sex.

Stories of children of the incarcerated

A JOINT PUBLICATION OF HERSTORY WRITERS WORKSHOP AND PRISON FAMILIES ANONYMOUS

First American edition published by Herstory Writers Workshop, Inc. 2015

ISBN: 978-0-9893533-1-1

Front cover photo: Rachel Wiener
Heart behind bars logo represents Prison Families Anonymous

"The Longest Wait of My Life," by Katherine De la Cruz, first appeared in *Voices: Memoirs from Herstory inside Long Island's Correctional Facilities*, published by Herstory Writers Workshop in 2012.

Herstory Writers Workshop, Inc.
2539 Middle Country Rd. FL 2
Centereach, New York 11720
Phone: 631-676-7395
Fax: 631-676-7396
www.herstorywriters.org

CONTENTS

Erika Duncan

FOREWORD

"All my life, God, I was on my knees having private conversations with You and hoping that You heard me, but did You? . . . At four years old, asking where Daddy was; five years old, same question; six years old, same question; until the events came—Daddy–Daughter teas in kindergarten, where I was the only one who showed up with my mom. Birthdays, Father's Day (waking up and wishing my mom Happy Father's Day.) . . .

". . . All I wanted was him to tuck me in when I was little. For him to pick me up and throw me in the air. For him to be on the empty side when I ran in the room and jumped on the bed because it was thundering outside. For him to be there at my Sweet Sixteen when it was time for the Daddy–Daughter dance. . . ."

Malaysia is one of the 2.7 million children living in the United States who have one or two parents in prison. The majority remain invisible, doing their best to blend in. They follow in the footsteps of their family members or legal guardians, who are trying to free them from stigma, keeping their losses and yearnings in the realm of their silent and most secret dreams. "When I was little, I remember my mom sitting at the kitchen table, scratching off the lottery (as usual), and I remember myself going up to her to ask her 'Where's my daddy?' and her exact words to me—a little six-year-old girl with pigtails and circular-type glasses, with a little hunch—'Your father is in the army. He left when you were one, and I don't think that he's coming home anytime soon.' It took Malaysia until she was twelve to learn that her father had been in prison all along. At sixteen—having passed that landmark birthday that she used to dream of—she still can't decide whether to research his crime on the internet or to wait until someone tells her about it more personally.

This collection of stories is intended to break the cycles of hiding, silencing and shame that are too often associated with children of the incarcerated. But beyond that it is meant to give voice to the yearning that is too often squelched, while giving a face to the brave young people who have lived with these feelings far too long, all alone.

"Still not living with any of my biological sisters," writes Tanasha, who at the age of seventeen decided to write a book about her experiences to help other people understand. "My mom, in jail, finally started writing me letters. Me, in shock because I didn't know what to write, how to feel, always had unconditional love for my mother. Me, in the church choir, loving to sing, happy, healthy . . . always wished my mother was there.

"Do you know how it feels to wonder if your mother is in jail? Dead? In the street? Coked up? There were times where I just wished my "mommy" never went to jail! Why my mommy? She is such a good person! Don't be mean to my mom! She doesn't deserve this! Imagine your mother in jail and she can't come see you because she has no freedom!"

"At the park I see all the dads pushing their kids on the swing set," writes Nicole. "When they get off I run and sit in the swing seat, wondering would my dad ever come and push me. I watch a lot of father–daughter movies and I run outside and I look up at the sky and ask God, 'What did I do not to deserve a father in my life?'

"When you cry, your father is able to catch your tears and he smiles at you and all of a sudden your tears disappear. But when I cry, my tears race down my face until they hit my cheeks and never stop, no one's there to wipe my tears away, so they dry up and that's where they always remain."

"My father would pick me up from my grandmother's house every day," writes Antisha. "One day when I was six, he didn't show up. Later that day, my mother told me he went to 'school.' I believed it for a while. A year or two later I caught on. I found out he was in jail. When I spoke on the phone with him he would constantly say, "I'll be home." I believed him till five years passed . . . I feel that it's his fault, why I am missing a part of my heart that hasn't been completely developed. Then again, people make mistakes. I won't give up on him, neither would I throw him under the bus."

* * *

Once a week after school, the young people whose stories you will read here came together to write with law interns from Touro Law Center and volunteers from Tikkun, an organization dedicated to restorative justice, following the notion that if they could tell their stories powerfully enough, they might dare a reading stranger to care. They worked with a team of older people, with Rachel Weiner, their beloved social worker and mentor, who heads the Center for Peace at Central Islip High School, who began to write her own story in the workshop, and with Barbara Allan, who had founded Prison Families Anonymous forty years prior, who was writing a book about what led her, as a lonely young mother of two whose husband had committed a horrific crime, to begin to form bonds with the families she saw in prison visiting rooms, to offer support, resources and family where too often there was none. They wrote with me and Serena Liguori of Herstory Writers Workshop, an organization dedicated to giving voice to some of Long Island's most vulnerable populations, including women and adolescent girls in jail, women in domestic violence shelters, and high school students coming from neighborhoods where gang violence, addiction, teen pregnancy, discrimination and incarceration were disproportionately high.

As you read, you will notice certain patterns and themes, as one by one the students come into their voices and dare to tell their truths. You will notice the movement from the expectation when they were very young children, to the gradual sobering and disappointment, even when some of the parents eventually came home. As you experience Desmond's recreating the way he experienced things as very young child, when the police raided his house and took his brother away, when he decided he would only be safe when he took the kitchen knife to school, you will cry along with these young people, and for a few moments you will become them in your hearts. You will become Destiny, as she is suddenly called by a stranger who introduces herself as her new stepmother, while telling her that her father is in jail, as you try to imagine the strength it took on the part of these children to navigate their lives. You will join in Aysha's recreation of her father—"name known from the east side of Long Island to the west. He's proud he's made a name for himself. Ganglord, number-one trapper, coolest guy around, am I right? He's a thug, childish gang-banger mentality, shit never gets old. In his mind he thinks he'll never live to twenty-one, so who cares what the hell he does?"—as she leads you through the imagined one-night stand after which—"Nine months later I pop out my mom and there I am." You will read two chapters of a book in progress by Shanequa, a writer with Herstory who is now in her thirties, in which she recreates the voice of the child learning about her world.

But mostly you will experience the spirit of these young people, their hopes and their dreams. As you move into the stories of the college writers, you will hear the same themes, but with more reflections and more emphasis on the dreams that could not be, as you read the stories of Amanda and Katherine, which culminate with their graduations, in which they are forced once again to find separation and peace.

It is our hope at Herstory, as we publish this book in partnership with Prison Families Anonymous, that it will be passed around from hand to hand, in the waiting rooms and visiting rooms of prisons, in parenting classes in prisons and jails, and in schools throughout our nation, where teachers and counselors must begin to understand the realities of the lives that so many of their students are leading. We hope that children of the incarcerated will find it, and that it will help them begin to come out of the sense of shame and isolation that has plagued so many of their lives. We hope that this book will help open hard conversations when parents come home, so that they can truly see how their children were feeling. And finally we hope that each writer in this book will be able to maintain the strength she or he began to gather in telling these stories on the page.

Tanasha Y. Gordon

INTRODUCTION

"A minor setback is only a test for a major comeback"

Have you ever thrown in the towel? Have you ever been so driven so far down the fast lane you've lost control? NO? Then you might want to read this book. You might want to take a jog in some of us young writers' shoes . . . Given the art of writing, learning the importance of intelligence and seeing the vision for which it stands, it seems like you give but the world takes. It seems like the ones you love best are the ones that hurt you the most. It seems as if you can never win. But that's not what it is. That's not right. You know why? Because each of these writers I have been working with for two years now has overcome one thing or another.

I first met them my senior year of high school, where I was a new student leaving Walt Whitman High School to go to Central Islip High School. The students I've written alongside don't even know they have overcome their minor setbacks. And by writing, it has set them up for their major comebacks. Writing with each of these writers from HERSTORY was not only was fun, exciting, but it was and still is inspirational and brought us so close together we formed a bond, a family.

A lot of the pieces you will read are about father figures and what a "father figure" should be, and NO MATTER WHAT, once they come home from prison, they should never—I repeat, NEVER—leave their children behind. I for one agree and relate to that. Now, being a nineteen-year-old mother living the same-sex lifestyle, I can only imagine how different my life would be–TOTALLY different—if I had a father figure.

How many more smiles I could have had than secret cries. I've always dreamed of what it would be like to have Mommy and Daddy together. Daddy coming home from work, buying his princess whatever she wanted, kissing Mommy and telling her how beautiful she was . . . That's how it's supposed to be, right? Well in my world it wasn't. It was such a loving "Mommy" in and out of jail, and "Daddy" just never there. Never there to wipe my tears. Never there to hold his baby girl and tell her everything would be okay. "Daddy is that you?" My life has consisted of hopeless dreams and broken promises.

A lot of these writers you are going to come across know the feeling. We have lived life with everyone saying we weren't going to be anything. We would never amount to anything. But now look who's reading OUR stories. Some people told me having my baby would be a setback. But little did they know my little angel was my major comeback!!

So let us introduce ourselves . . .

A SEARCH
FOR THE
TRUTH

Nicole Annmarie Mauvais

A Father Figure

Nicole was the free spirit of our high school workshop, wearing her feelings on her sleeve both in her writing and in her response to the other students in the group. She wrote many vivid chapters, rich in dialogue and introspection, chronicling the search for her real father and the various confusions and bumps on the way, so that we all waited for the next leg of her story. She has chosen only to share her opening prose poem for this collection.

Can you tell me how it feels to have a dad? Can you tell me how it feels to know the exact location he stays at? How does it feel to know your dad is able to watch you grow? How does it feel to know that your dad doesn't come into your life for a quick minute and then he goes? Are you able to sleep at night because you know your dad is sleeping in the bed right across the hall?

Do you cry because he works late once a month? I need to know, when you fall do you get up and cry or run to your dad to show him your cut? I want to know because I don't think my biological father ever comforted me not once.

At the park I see all the dads pushing their kids on the swing set. When they get off I run and sit in the swing seat, wondering would my dad ever come and push me? I watch a lot of father–daughter movies and I run outside and I look up at the sky and ask God, "What did I do not to deserve a father in my life?"

When you cry, your father is able to catch your tears and he smiles at you and all of a sudden your tears disappear. But when I cry, my tears race down my face until they hit my cheeks and never stop, no one's there to wipe my tears away, so they dry up, and that's where they always remain.

In your dad's mind you're a Daddy's little girl. In my father's mind, I know he wishes I was never born, but I really didn't ask to be here. These questions remain in my head unanswered, waiting for my father to come around.

I sit outside and pull flowers out of the ground and I realize I'm just like a flower, because without soil a flower is unable to grow and will soon die out. A girl without a father has no one to show her love and no one to protect her.

So I lie on my bed with the flower under my pillow and ask myself will I die without a father–daughter relationship, just like the yellow flower without the soil.

And I dream about having a father figure when I was little. There's only one problem: that father figure wasn't my biological dad; it was my stepdad, playing and acting like he was my biological father.

When I found out he wasn't my real dad, the truth tore my heart apart. Do you know what it feels like to find out the man you grew up knowing as your dad really isn't your dad? I wasn't just mad or sad. I was confused. I didn't know what to do.

How much suffering do I have to go through for my biological father to see and realize my pain? Why should I have to suffer and be the one that's upset? Why do I have to be one of the little girls that always has her head down explaining to people that I have a deadbeat dad.

So how does it feel to have love from your dad? 'Cause that's the only thing I wish I had.

Malaysia G.

My Survival Guide

For many weeks Malaysia hid behind giggling and running interference about the seriousness of the workshop, until one day she surprised us with this very full narrative that combines heartbreak, an amazingly mature way of looking at her own feelings at various ages, and an ongoing sense of storyline. As soon as she put her heart into the project, she became one of the group's most prolific writers.

2010

Some may say that living without their father isn't that bad, or that they don't need him in their life to survive at all, because they learned how to do things without him. Well to me, a girl who's lived and learned without her father in her life for sixteen years thinks otherwise. A girl without her father is like a scale without notes or a song without lyrics . . . EMPTY. But somehow I have a bond with a man that I barely know . . . and that bond has only just begun. But the real question replaying itself in my head is, *will he look the way I pictured him to look in my head? Will we have the same features like everyone says we do?* I don't know.

When I was little, I remember my mom sitting at the kitchen table scratching off the lottery (as usual), and I remember myself going up to her to ask her, "Where's my daddy?" and her exact words to me . . . a little six-year-old girl with pigtails and circular-type glasses, with a little hunch: "Your father is in the army. He left when you were one, and I don't think that he's coming home anytime soon." I was six, so I kind of believed it until two years later when I was eight years old and I began to get restless on waiting for a big man with an army suit to walk through my door to greet me with a hug and tell me everything's okay, he's home now. But I guess for an eight-year-old, my imagination was pretty big.

I wanted to know so much about him, so I began to ask around the family. I asked my two aunts, my uncle, my grandpa, grandma and everyone I could think of. I've been asking around for about four years . . .

* * *

Twelve years old and I finally found out the truth about a lie that led me on. I got a call from my Nana Carol asking me to come down to Alabama with my family for the summer. Now I didn't know about them and I instantly thought, *Oh no, hillbillies and farms and poop,* and just knew I was not that type of girl. But when she said, "Your father's sister and his nieces and his mother would love to see you and how big you've gotten," I lit up with joy to think, FINALLY, after years after years of searching it felt so good . . .

So that summer came along and I was on my way to Alabama driving (by the way longest drive EVER). I had butt aches sitting for that long, even though we stopped at rest stops and stuff. BUT ANY-WAY, when we finally got there to this nice one-story tan brick house with cute little garden gnomes and lights lining the walkway and a whole bunch of cars that lined the block, I figured I'd wait to get to where I was staying before jumping into things.

The party was packed with family I'd never seen in my life. They were hugging me and kissing my face and just showering me with love. I'd swear I was a celebrity or something. But after the party ended and I finally got to relax at the house, everyone left and my cousin, I guess, showed me to the room I'd be staying in for the summer. My nana (Daddy's mom) came into the room and welcomed me with a big hug and telling me I'd got so big since she'd last seen me. That's when I asked, "When was that?" and she told me when I was about an infant. I thought to myself, WELL DUH, *I was a baby, I'm twelve now, what a dummy*. But I didn't hold back on asking her about my father, since we were alone.

She told me how funny he was and how much I looked like him and that he's tall and skinny and blah, blah, blah. I didn't care at that moment. All I wanted to know was where he was. So I asked softly, not fast, about being anxious, and she took a deep breath and said, "I guess I should tell you now." She said that I was at that age where I deserved to know.

She started off with "They took him." *Who took him? . . . took him where? Well, call them and tell them to bring him back* was all I was thinking, but I said nothing but "Who?" She told me, "The bad guys," and I was getting upset already. I told her, "The bad guys? Really? Nana, I'm twelve, you don't have to kiddy-talk with me." So she told me the whole entire story about how when I was born he got sent to jail . . . just jail, and how he got let out and he came home up until I was one, when he got sent to prison.

She said that she wasn't going to tell me what he did because she didn't want me to feel afraid of him. She said that before he left he gave her something to give to me and it was his ring. Inside that ring was a picture of me and my big brother. I shed a tear. She continued and told me that when I was a baby they took me to visit him and that he held me and he cried until visiting hours were over. She said she couldn't tell me nothing else, so she said goodnight to me and left the room.

I went to bed that night crying, just because I knew he was thinking about me wherever he was and he was alive and he missed me. I also went to bed disappointed at the fact that my mother lied to me . . . I mean I guess I was too young to know . . . BUT STILL.

That morning I got woken up by my nana telling me to sit up and drink some orange juice. She spoke "Hold onto the house phone," and gave it to me. Thinking that it was my mom calling to check up on me. I said, "Yeah, Ma?" and a deep, manly voice said, "Try again." I said, "Who is this?" He replied, "Think hard, Baby Girl." "Just tell me," I said, "or I'm gonna hang up in three, two, one . . ."

"It's Daddy, Baby Girl. It's Daddy."

My eyes filled like a glass of water and poured out tears because to hear his voice shook my heart and I didn't know what to say I was so speechless . . . "Daddy?"

* * *

WINTER 2015

As I watched all of the inmates walk out, I put my head down because I could identify which one was my dad. My hands started trembling, my leg was shaking uncontrollably. I was staring down at the floor because I was scared to look up at the man I'd last seen when I was a baby, a toddler.

What if he doesn't have anything to say to me? . . . What if he can't even look at me? I saw white sneakers standing there and I couldn't look up at him because I let my nerves get the best of me.

"Laysia?" he said. His voice sounded just like it did on the phone. He grabbed my hand and pulled me up to hug him, but I closed my eyes because I wasn't ready to look at him yet. Wow, he's tall.

I wrapped my hands around his neck and let all my tears flow out. Once we finished our hug, I kept my eyes closed to ready myself to look at the mystery man, because that's what I called him, because I didn't know what he looked like.

Well, here I go, opening them in three, two, one!

There he was, standing there, a skyscraper with a faded haircut, eyebrows stood out to me, they looked like big black caterpillars, his dark brown eyes filled with tears. But I couldn't tell whether they were of joy or sadness. He had a little beard I could see growing in. He wore navy blue pants and a matching button-up shirt with a number on it. It was so hard to look at him this way.

The first five minutes of the visit were mostly staring and crying. But once we got to talking, it was like we were best friends who'd been away from each other for a while but had so much to talk about. He smiled and laughed, a laugh that was pretty contagious. But I loved it. Everyone was saying how much we looked alike feature-wise. I could see it—his eyes, lips and nose, ugh that's why my nose was so huge!

After laughing for a while about how much we looked alike, we finally got down to talking about the basics, as if we were on the phone. He told me about the days he wanted to kick someone's behind because they were testing him, but all he had to do was think about coming home to me and he would relax and return to his "comfort zone." Like he said for some reason I couldn't stop staring at him. I wanted the image of him to stay in my head forever! I didn't wanna forget him ever . . . he was my dad. And what if I never get a chance to visit him again? Which I wouldn't because I knew my mom wasn't going to allow me to go places with my stepmom. So just in case, I sat there taking pictures in my mind and storing them in this little section I have where all the thoughts about him were.

I asked so many questions that I'd been thinking of asking him since forever. But there was one question I wanted to ask ever since I was twelve. I could've asked him on the phone, but I was scared then and I put it to the back of my mind. But sitting here in front of him brought it back to the tip of my tongue. I asked him, "What did you do that caused them to lock you away for so long?"

He let his head fall and I could see that he was nervous because he couldn't stop fiddling with his fingers. I moved next to him and I put my head on his shoulder and told him that it was okay and that whatever it was didn't matter to me, because I loved him, and nothing could change the way I felt about my dad.

It looked like he was scared to say it and I didn't want to make him feel uncomfortable, so I changed the subject. He told me about my baby days and how much work I was. He apologized for going away, but I knew it wasn't his fault so I didn't really acknowledge it. But that's where I stopped . . . because half of this, or mainly all of this was his fault. If he hadn't been out on the streets, as my mom said, being a player—player and etc.—he wouldn't have been in the position that he was in right now! But, I couldn't let him know that I thought that. It was just a thought anyway. Still, never changed the way I felt.

We talked about everything we couldn't get to in our letters. He was telling me about the birds and the bees—in other words, sex and falling in love. I was nodding my head and smiling the whole time, but thinking, *You're a little too late to have this talk with me*, which I don't know why because he knew about my boyfriend and how long I'd been with him. I'd told him everything in the letters about us, but he still continued to talk.

Thirty minutes of visiting hours left . . . I had thirty minutes to cram in everything I wanted to tell him. I cried while telling him about life at home: the relationships with my mom, my brother and everyone else in my life, how some left me confused, upset, lonely and insignificant. But sitting there with him made me feel like I was never any of these things. I didn't wanna end the visit in tears, so I began asking him how the food was because I knew it wasn't fried chicken, pork chops and steak. He laughed. There goes that laugh again.

Realizing that our thirty minutes were coming to an end, I couldn't help but cry again. I thought over this being my last time seeing him. He put his arms around me, causing all my tears to be soaked up into his shirt. I told him through my jittery voice that I didn't wanna leave. Yes, I was acting like I was twelve again. He wiped my tear off of my face and told me, "Don't think of this a good-bye, think of it as hello."

That buzzer rang again, letting me know that all the inmates were being rounded back to their cells—I guess—if that's what they called it. As soon as he let go of my hand I began to cry hysterically. He looked back at me and mouthed "hello." It took me a while to figure out why we were leaving and were saying hello.

But I forgot this wasn't goodbye, so I mouthed back "hello" and turned to leave with my stepmom.

✳ ✳ ✳

Every day I ask God, "Why did it have to be me? Why did You have to give me a life of struggle, lies and confusion? Why did I have to be the one out of many fatherless kids? I'm not ungrateful. I don't necessarily hate my life, but I just want to know why. Why did I have to live off of lies I've been told? Why did I have to have lost hopes? When I prayed to You on the lonely nights I lay awake thinking about him and how he was doing, asking You to bring him home to me. Practically begging You to hold his hand through his parole hearing, hoping they would reopen his case and see that he has changed, he has learned his lesson.

"All my life, God, I was on my knees having private conversations with You and hoping that You heard me, but did You? From what I was told, I began to clearly talk when I was four. At four years old, asking where Daddy was; five years old, same question; six years old, same question; until the events came—Daddy–Daughter teas in kindergarten, where I was the only one who showed up with my mom. Birthdays, Father's Day (waking up and wishing my mom Happy Father's Day, and my father a happy belated). It just feels weird to be watching TV and then something on the TV snaps me into a depressing mood.

Everyone has it all—well some people. All I wanted was him to tuck me in when I was little. For him to pick me up and throw me in the air. For him to be on the empty side when I ran into the room and jumped on the bed because it was thundering outside. For him to be there at my Sweet Sixteen when it was time for the Daddy- Daughter dance, but instead I didn't have one. I wanted nothing at my Sweet Sixteen to remind me of him and be upset for the night. Plus my makeup was on track.

"I don't know when he's coming home. I don't feel like I should have to live with these thoughts that eat away at me in the night anymore. So God, if You are there, I'm asking You, I am begging You to bring him home. I miss him too much. I think about him too much. I love him so much. I know we don't all get what we want, but I'm really fed up with the way that my life is, and the sharp turn it's taking. I'm not as happy as I come off to be. I go through a lot for my age and I'm fed up. I stress about so much that I might be shaking hands with You sooner that You know."

Tanasha Y. Gordon

The Day I Call "Why?"

Tanasha—or "Tee," as she likes to be called—knew right away that she wanted to write a book that would help others to walk in her shoes. She began the first chapter even before our workshop had properly begun, each week adding a new episode or reflection as she alternated between odes to survival and heartbreaking passages about despair. She has read her work extensively in public as part of Herstory's justice program. As she enters motherhood, she is proud of her same-sex relationship and intent upon raising her daughter in a very different way.

Do you know what it's like to not have a father not be able to play basketball with you? Parents to take you shopping? Do you know what it's like to have parents in jail and they cannot provide for you financially? I used to play basketball around the corner as a kid with my closest friend, Kay-tee. Her dad would give her money. Her mom would see what she wanted to eat. Her dad would even come play basketball with her sometimes. But, what about me? I never had a father to play basketball or football with. Never had a mommy to ask what a period was, or sex.

What do you know about your mother and father? I cannot tell you what my mother's favorite drink is. I can maybe tell you her full name and favorite color. I don't even know how old my parents are. Now, think about everything you know about your parents. I wish I had my real mother and father to tell me what to do, give me rules.

This not only should give you an outlook on how one can be affected by parents that have been in trouble with the law, it should also make you realize and appreciate your parents, whether it is just your mother or your father, because seventeen-year-olds like me would LOVE to take your place.

✳ ✳ ✳

Jail . . . it will get you . . . it will mold you . . . it will shape you . . . But it will never take the pain away that I have felt most of my seventeen years of life. It affected me much! I felt alone. I felt like all the other boys and girls had mommies and daddies, but I didn't. I had people who played the role, but that cannot replace the feeling that I had. Sometimes, I just walked around with a frown, just wanted to punish things and throw things.

Some people wonder how I became such a good person, how I didn't end up in trouble or a juvenile delinquent. It was only God that has kept me mentally sane. But when you see someone or try to judge someone, look at their background, find out their history. Being a child to a parent that is in jail is not easy. Before you criticize anyone, find out about their book and the story inside it.

Daddy, is that you?

✳ ✳ ✳

Still not living with any of my biological sisters. My mom, in jail, finally started writing me letters. Me, in shock because I didn't know what to write, how to feel, always had unconditional love for my mother. Me, in the church choir, loving to sing, happy, healthy . . . always wished my mother was there.

Do you know how it feels to wonder if your mother is in jail? Dead? In the street? Coked up? There were times where I just wished my mommy never went to jail! Why my mommy?! She is such a good person! Don't be mean to my mom! She doesn't deserve this! Imagine your mother in jail and she can't come see you because she has no freedom!

Daddy, is that you?

✳ ✳ ✳

Mommy, coming to visit me at times. I don't remember how often over the weekends, but whenever she did, I never wanted her to leave. Now, eight years old, spoke up for myself and said, "I want to live with my mommy." Did I get to go? Yes, of course. But, did it last long? Hell, no! I used to go to my Aunt Mary's house with bruises and cuts on my arms and legs from getting beaten. Did I think anything of it? No, because I loved my mommy. She is a good person. I didn't want anything to happen to her.

Three months . . . three months is as long as it lasted. Everything had gotten so bad that we had to go back to court for custody battle. Me, in the courtroom, not knowing what was happening, just sat there, hour after hour after hour, waiting for my mom. Soon, Mom storming out of the room, turning the corner and sitting on the floor. Me, looking at her with a sweet benevolent smile as she says, "DON'T LOOK AT ME." With tears in my eyes, Why can't I look at my mommy? I love her. Why is she being so mean to me? She is a good person. I know she doesn't mean it.

Later on, around eight o'clock, "Come on, Tanasha, it is time to go." My mother, angry and tears in her eyes, me, walking with my "mom," who has raised since the age of two. This day—I always remember it as "the day before Thanksgiving." My first holiday with my mother was soon to be destroyed, and I know why . . . but that's a different story.

Then, not too long after, my "mom" tells me, "Your mother is in jail." Wow! The sharp pain I felt in my heart. I wanted to go visit her but was too scared to ask.

All this I am telling you is brand new to everyone. No one EVER knew I felt this way. No one EVER knew I had this pain . . . no one but my Aunt Mary.

∗ ∗ ∗

The most precious angel I can imagine, the glow of my day—the perfect reflection of a saint. I loved her with all my heart and might. She was my backbone, my anchor. When I would get in trouble I would hear her say, "Leave that girl alone, Purr," her lovely way of saying her sister's name. She knew my secrets in and out. She knew what I was going to do before or even while I was doing it. She had my heart. If it wasn't Aunt Mary, it wasn't anybody.

I stayed with her for about three weeks before I went back with my "mom." Her house was the one everyone ran to in their time of need, in their time of trouble, maybe even just to say some kind words or expression like "Thank you," "I love you." Every time my mom would say, "Get on your shoes, we goin' to Sista's house!" ("Sista" was what she called her) I jumped up, grabbed my shoes and hurried up out the door, forgetting my hair was not done or I was still in my pajamas that I changed into every day I came home from school. I loved coming from church and my mom stopping at the stop sign, me, in excitement, waiting for that left-turn blink to come on. And when it did, I couldn't help but smile, trying to hide my excitement, trying to rush my mom out the car. At times when I didn't hear that blinker, I would make an excuse, "Maybe she cooked dinner . . . maybe she needs help with something."

At times, I loved to hear that car pull up in front of my house, I could always tell when she pulled up, her nice pretty shiny white van had a certain sound it made, a distinctive sound, a sound that no one else could make. Until one day, that left-turn blinker turned into no blinker at all and that sound could no longer be heard . . . the day I call "Why?"

✳ ✳ ✳

Waking up that morning, taking extra long to get ready for school. Wanting to see my Aunt Mary, something telling me, go, go, go! So I decided I was going to take my cousin's bus since his bus came a little later than mine.

Phone rings. Caller ID: *Mary.* I quickly jump to answer the phone, but my older brother, Jared, got to it first. I listened for a moment, realizing it was just my cousins goofing around, laughing, soon realizing that laugh I was hearing was a sorrowful cry from her daughter.

Jared running upstairs, saying repeatedly, "I have to go to Aunt Mary's house," me asking, "Can I go? Can I go?" He says, "No" as I fix my lips to ask, "Why?" He says, "She stopped breathing." Me, gasping for air, "Oh, no!" Then, not too soon after, putting a smile on my face: *That's Aunt Mary, she will be okay.*

Jared running up and down the steps, trying to get himself together. I ask, "Should I call Mommy?" He pauses and says, "Yeah." By the look on his face, I could see this was more serious than I thought. He left. I called my mom's job, speaking to her boss, whose name was also Mary. "Oh, my God! I will tell her when she comes back." My other brother, Devon, running out the room. I tell him what's going on. Him, getting ready to get Mom from work—she still has two hours before she gets back to the yard. Soon hearing the phone ring. From the way he was talking, I could tell it was Jared. Me, saying in my head, "Ah, she is okay!"

Devon breaks down his voice sounding raspy, "No, man, don't tell me that! Don't tell me that! No!" Only one thing that could mean . . . she was gone. Devon, finally getting off the phone, goes to get Mom as I call all my uncles. Devon pulls up, I run outside, get in the car and there we go, on our way to the hospital. Everyone crying. I sit in the waiting room.

My other aunt comes out and asks, "Do you want to see her?" I walk in the room of Huntington Hospital and see her lying there peacefully, tears in my eyes, my mom and two brothers surrounding her. MY AUNT MARY IS GONE! Everyone blaming themselves, blaming each other for things they could not do. Me, blaming myself because if I would have left when I first walked out that door, I would have been able to save her. Realizing the day before, I missed the bus and was mad at her for not being able to take me. There are so many parts missing, but cannot be described in detail. Aunt Mary was gone, the matron of the family gone. And that is where everyone's life changed.

Antisha Townsend

Who Is There to Blame?

Antisha threw herself into the writing right away. She was the first in the workshop to explore what it was like to be a child being told false stories and soon became an inspiration for the others who had similar tales. She was able to continue adding new sections as her father came home, and shared a public reading with him in a very moving way. She wants to be a lawyer someday.

My father hasn't been here.
  Who is there to blame?
In and out them fucking bars,
  like this is a game.
Haven't been here so long,
  starting to forget his name.
God only know my pain,
  sorry to speak his name in vain
I got a future to obtain,
  this shit isn't a game.

I hope he realize he got a life to change.
Cause all these gang banging ain't provin' a thing.
I hope he jump back in the right damn lane.

y father would pick me up from my grandmother's house every day. One day when I was six, he didn't show up. Later that day, my mother told me he went to "school." I believed it for a while. A year of two later I caught on. I found out he was in jail. When I spoke on the phone with him he would constantly say "I'll be home soon." I believed him till five years passed. I was eleven years old. Every birthday I would receive a letter from him. Every letter I read, I began to cry. The feeling of an absent father is really hard to deal with. I always dreamed of attending a father–daughter dance, but there can't be a father–daughter dance without the father. I miss the hugs and kisses that I used to get. Nine years of an absent father really hurts. I almost feel as if I was ABANDONED. I feel that it's his fault, why I am missing a part of my heart that hasn't been completely developed. Then again, people make mistakes. I won't give up on him; neither would I throw him under the bus.

My mother constantly tells me how much he didn't do for me. No child like me wants to hear their parent trying to bring up negative things about someone they truly love. I hate when people call him a deadbeat. I feel he tries. He says he will improve when he gets home. I have hope. I truly love my father, whether he has been here or not. One day I will grow up to have children. I would do anything to make sure they won't go through what I'm going through now.

✳ ✳ ✳

Beep. Beep. Beep. (Sound of metal detector.) My sister, my mom and I were all dressed up, hair done and tired from the long ride there. My mother was told she had to take apart her hair, because she had bobby pins holding in her hairstyle. She wasn't very happy about it, but she did it for my sister and me.

It took forever to get to see him, it was a very long process. Taking off shoes, taking out beads and bobby pins—we even had to fill out paperwork and wait on lines. When I first walked in the door, I spotted my father at my first glance. My sister was young, so she wasn't really sure how he looked. I ran to him to give him a hug. Then he had to be behind a counter for the visit. The counter had no glass; it wasn't what I expected at all. I was extremely happy to see him.

I don't remember our conversation but I know the voice of my father really brightened my day. The struggle we went through to enter didn't quite matter anymore. What was important was that I finally got to see my dad. He had been absent for about nine years.

Hopefully he comes out like he told me he would. If not then, I'll have to see him next year, his original release date. I just hope to see my father soon, not only for myself but for my little sisters as well—two twelve-year-olds and an eight-year-old. They need him more than I do. Well, I will continue waiting like I have been doing my whole life.

* * *

I'm glad I never gave up on hope. I kept it up for nine years. People doubted him. People said I was stupid for believing him. Well I wasn't, he is finally back. Now I have a chance to bond with my father. I am more happy than before. I can finally walk around with confidence, knowing I have two parents to comfort me when I'm upset or need someone to talk to. Just having my father back really makes me happy.

Monday afternoon I was told he was being picked up from the jail by my grandmother. I was excited, my mother drove my sister and me to my grandmother's house and there we were. I ran upstairs, seeing my father in the room, watching TV. He looked the same as when he left. I didn't really say much, because I was so excited that I ran out of words. I sat there waiting for my other sisters to arrive. Next thing you knew, we had a house full of people and kids running around the house. After all, my dream of that father–daughter dance finally might come true. I'm just patiently waiting for my Sweet Sixteen to come.

* * *

It's been almost a month since my father has been home. I've seen him about five times. He calls me about three times a week. Seeing "Daddy" pop up on my phone makes me happy. When I go to my grandmother's house instead of going to my older sister's room, I go to my father's room. I don't really talk to him about much. When I go out, he asks me where I am going, who I'm going with. Usually I get annoyed when people ask me a lot of questions, but being that he is trying to look out and fill in the blank part of my life he missed, I guess it's okay. Soon my mother and father will be planning my Sweet Sixteen, the thing I have always been waiting for. The moment I've dreamed of a part of my life I hoping I would never forget. Having a father actually really makes me a happier person.

* * *

Like I said, my dreams were pages ripped out of a fairytale book. My father isn't the father I thought I would have. I don't even know him. I see him but, to be honest, I know nothing about him. Already having another sibling—that's not at all what I wanted. He can't even properly take care of the ones he has already. All he thinks about is his hoes, which one he going to see that day. Well, I don't care anymore. I was brought up without a father. There is no need to depend on one just because he is around. If he can't grow up and do what he has to do, I guess he is just another person taking an unreliable spot in my life.

AYSHA M.

The 39th Parallel

From the beginning Aysha liked mystery and hidden meanings. Whenever we'd ask for more clarity she would counter that it was up to the reader to understand. When we asked her about the title for her piece, she pointed out that "during the Korean War, Korea was separated into two, the North and the South. The line that separated the North from the South was called the 38th parallel." She explained her life as being the 39th parallel, separated into two: her father living in jail, on one side, and she living in the outside world, on the other. Aysha has spoken about her dreams of becoming a marine biologist and/or an art therapist—different dreams on different days.

Rashid, the name known from the east side of Long Island to the west. He's proud he's made a name for himself. Gang lord, number-one trapper, coolest guy around, am I right? He's a thug, childish gang-banger mentality, shit never gets old. In his mind he thinks he'll never live to twenty-one, so who cares what the hell he does? He's a lone wolf, runs the streets from twelve in the afternoon to four in the A.M. Smokes a blunt at least twice a day. Chillin' in the streets, rolling with the rest of the thugs.

He meets up with the usual crew of girls that also chill on west side. This time there's a new face, pretty white girl with light eyes. He gets to know her, they have some typical thug love story type of romance going on. One day he's in the car with her and she throws up on the side of the road, she claims she's sick. Next day she calls him on the phone with an "I'm pregnant". That's where this shit all began.

Nine months later I pop out of my mom and there I am. Rashid is there, grandmother, close relatives, I don't really know. All I know is, that's the day a father should have become a father. Now obviously this didn't happen. He eventually within a year, still chillin' with the same no-good thugs, gets arrested in some type of robbery. He claims he had no part, but his ass was there so he got the penalty for it.

He's sentenced to some time in jail. Not sure how long, but I know it's not his first time in there. My mom who just had me is now a single parent, and I might add, not the best. She eventually disappears on me too. I say "too" because when Rashid got out of jail, his ass never came back. You'd think a man in jail knowing he got a baby girl out there somewhere would come find her and be a father. Well, I guess we all got it wrong. I guess a few years in jail wasn't enough time away, so he went looking for some more time. When you got a disappearing mother and a jailbird named Rashid, this life already has a shit start.

My ma came back two years before Rashid, finally when I was eight. That's when he returned, now just a bum living on my ma's couch. Now I ain't the only kid he had. Three months before my birth was my brother's birth. We don't have the same ma but we're still close. I got lucky though, I had an uncle around to take me in and show me the ropes of life. Not saying it was easy, but it wasn't terrible. As for my brother, he's just like my dad, bad-ass kid thinking he a man, growing up the wrong way: weed, gangs, old thugs recruiting.

I knew better than to listen when Rashid told me something about his past and jail. I guess my brother didn't. We used to sit in front of the couch while my father sat on it. He'd tell us about his drug deals and the hood and running from the cops, getting stabbed, all the years leading up to now. My brother soaked in all these stories, which weren't the best because all Rashid told you was how to get in jail, not how to not be like him and actually go to college and to live a life crime free.

I'm not going to sit here and act like I don't have some of Rashid's mentality. I've had a trip into the troubled land, but I got more brains over all his gene and traits crap, so I corrected myself.

Aside from all this background explaining and flashbacks, in between these six hundred and seventy-six words, have you noticed once that there's a father missing? Maybe so, but if you ain't never had one you wouldn't think twice about it. A father.

Destiny

"I Know You Don't Know Me..."

It was Destiny's serious side that she let us see first. From the very beginning her writing explored secrets and their impact on the people involved, with her stories always involving many players and scenes. She enjoyed rearranging the pieces of her story, so that it would tell more. This is just a piece of a much longer work.

Do you know what it's like to live without your father? Well, I've never ever lived with mine. He was in and out of my life. He would be gone for years and then reappear again. But only this time he appeared with a new girl in his life and that girl wasn't my sister.

It all started with a phone call. Ring! Ring! Ring! I answered.

"Hi," said this strange, soft, kind voice. "Is this Destiny?"

"Yes," I responded. Who is this?"

"Hi, Destiny, my name is Sequoia and I'm going to be your step-mother."

I at the age of eight screamed at her, "I don't need another mom!" I always believed my dad and mom would work it out.

"Des, I'm sorry and I know you don't know me, but I would never do anything to harm you."

"Where's my dad? I want to talk to him, I'll change his mind."

"Destiny, sweetheart, your dad is away right now. He won't be home until next year."

"Oh? What? Where is he?" I asked, hearing her voice tremble.

She lowly responded and said, "Sweetheart, your daddy isn't a bad guy, but he is in a place where bad people go. Okay? Everything will be okay. It was just a misunderstanding."

"My dad is in jail? And I'm going to have a stepmom? What's next?"

* * *

A blessing, my protector, my provider, my mother. She took such good care of my siblings and me. And she sacrificed everything for us. We have everything we need in life and were taught so much. She's there for us when we need her, even at our worst. But I witnessed my mom crying a lot. We had a type of mother–daughter relationship like no other. We would talk about things in her life and what she was going through. Things at the time, I just didn't understand, but she knew I would listen.

"Destiny, everything seems fine, but to be honest with you, it's not. I know you hear that Dunor and I are arguing and fighting a lot. We're getting a divorce."

I, at the age of nine, wasn't quite sure what that meant, but I listened as she cried and told me more. "Things aren't working for us and we are apart."

Seeing my mom cry wasn't the best thing in the world. As she went through a long, harsh divorce, she cried. Everything was put on her.

* * *

Now I'm eighteen and a recent conversation with my mom really made me think. I cried as she was telling me everything she's dealing with. I realized that with the job that I have, I'm not able to help my mom. She's dealing with problems with the house. Everything seems to be falling apart, one thing after the other.

"Des, I can't do this anymore. No one is wanting to help me. I'm trying, Des, I am." Tears rolling down my mom's face and pain filling my heart. I have to try to help her. She's my mom, she can't go through this on her own. My dad hasn't been around all my life, and the divorce left her alone.

CHILDHOOD MEMORIES

Desmond Mashon Leonard

Scared

Desmond came into the workshop with the announcement that "I promise to write you a big story." He became very intrigued with the art of writing in the voice of the child in order to take the reader "back there." This allowed him to share his journey out of the world he knew as a child in a very honest way that won the hearts of all who heard his work.

Hello, my name is Desmond Leonard. I remember one morning I woke up and I wasn't feeling too good and I was running a little bit late. I remember going on the bus and the kids were bothering me. Then when I got off the bus someone pushed me in the dirt where the flowers were. Everyone stopped and laughed at me. I went to the office crying, trying to call home, but no one answered. I had to walk around school with everyone calling me Dirty and Stinky. I cried. Then when I was outside and a group of boys walked up to me and told me, "We're going to jump you tomorrow." I was scared.

When I got home I went to my room to cry until my dad got home. I stopped like nothing happened. I was so upset and scared.

The next day I woke up scared and kept thinking about what was going to happen in school. Before I left I quickly grabbed a knife from the kitchen.

I was scared on the bus, very scared. The kids were bothering me on the bus and the bus driver blamed me and told me to come to the front. I was really scared, shaking. Then I heard a cry, "OMG he's going to kill us!" repeatedly. I was confused and wondering why she said that; then I realized the knife fell out of my pocket and I tried to quickly discard it in my bag.

Everyone was held on the bus and I was the only one who got off nervous and scared. I was in the office with a social worker, scared and shaking with fear and wondering what was going to happen. I was young, only eight or nine years old, in fourth grade, not knowing what was going to happen to me. They asked, "Did I have a weapon?" and I answered, staggering, saying, "Yessss," like I couldn't speak, breathless. My mom finally came and it felt like my heart was jumping out of my chest. I was scared. I started crying, even more scared, and I was asked and I burst out saying I was being bullied and every time I told someone, everyone took me as a joke and acted like they didn't care. I said angrily to them, "Now y'all take action when I bring a knife to school, but not all the times I was being bullied." I still had tears coming down my eyes. My mom and everyone said, "Sorry for not paying attention," but I still was suspended till further notice.

When I reached home with my mom that day she yelled at me for like five minutes till she broke down and cried to me, saying, "I'm sorry Des. I'm sorry," and hugged me saying, "I love you and I'm sorry."

* * *

The day I realized I hate police was when they barged in my house and made my dad cry. I was very scared. Waking up hearing my front door being run down. People running in the house, me waking up and my vision all blurred, not fully awake. Me still—haven't processed in my mind at a young age what's happening—scared. The officer yanked me by my arm aggressively and tossed me on the couch like I was some type of rag doll. My eyes open wide, me fully awakened at this point. My nephew Leeky was tossed on the couch next to me—him looking like someone stole something from him because he just woke up. My eyes wandering around the house, then turned towards my parent's room with my parents in handcuffs screaming, "What the fuck is happening?" They were told to be quiet and were placed on the couch next to me. My head rang a bell saying, *It's the police, but why are they here in my head?*

We heard screams, and it was my brother screaming, saying, "What's going on?" Leeky looked at me and I looked back at him and we both gave each other the face like "WTF" are we going thru? They finally yelled at my brother and told him to shut his freaking mouth and pushed him and his girlfriend on the couch. He finally kept calm and stopped talking. They said my name, "Desmond Mashon Leonard." I stood up and they said out loud, "Desmond has been seen with a firearm." My brother said, "Don't say anything to these pigs and keep your mouth shut." They told him to shut up—I still standing confused, wondering, *What's a firearm?* Then words started clicking together in my young mind, saying, *Oh, I don't have or own a firearm.*

They searched the house once more again and didn't find any guns but they did find drugs/weed in the house because of my brother. The officer told me and Leeky to stand up and come with them. My Dad told them to take us to our Aunt's house; she lives around the corner. My brother once again said, "Don't say anything to them fucking PIGS."

We are walking out the door and seeing a lot of police cars outside, about seven cop cars and two special unit trucks. We finally were in the cop car and finally pulled off—me looking back at my house, with flashing red, white and blue lights. I was sitting in the back seat, mad, and told the driving officers, "I hate cops" and "You guys are annoying," and sucked my teeth. My nephew Raliek tapped me and told me to shut up and grabbed my arm tightly until I calmed down. The officer started laughing like I was playing around.

We finally reached my Aunt's house and the officer said, "Let's go" and grabbed my arm tightly until I told him, "I am capable of walking," and he grabbed me tighter, and then I pushed him off of me and he gave me a look and I gave him one back.

My aunt told me to go inside and calm down and relax. My nephew followed me and I did as she wanted while she was talking to the officer. About twenty minutes later I went outside to ride my bike around, and I was thinking about going to ride to my house, but my aunt caught me and called me down and told me not to go down there. Ten minutes later I finally saw my dad's car coming, and he finally pulled up and got out of the car and hugged me tightly and started crying. Then he told me and my nephew to hop in the car, he'd be there in a second, with tears running down his face. He hugged his sister saying, "I never wanted to be embarrassed like this in front of my boys."

And they took Charles away (my brother). And I was shocked. My eyes popped out and I started crying myself, and so did Raliek, but I wasn't sad. It was all anger and I knew Leeky was mad because that's his dad. He put his arm over my shoulder and told me, "It's going to be all good and we'll be fine."

Shanequa Levin

The Stranger

This selection is part of a book in progress about Shanequa's coming-of-age journey in a world of poverty and racism, to be ready for publication in early 2016. Shanequa, director of Every Child Matters on Long Island and president of Long Island Mocha Moms, has been one of the most prolific writers attending Herstory's Bridges to Justice Workshop in Patchogue and is a deep believer in giving voice to children everywhere. Her nuanced portrait of her mother adds an important dimension to the literature of prison families and the strength that these matriarchs often bring to their children, despite their own trials and tribulations.

My father's been writing me letters from jail. When his letters come in the mail with my name on them, I get excited, but I don't let my mother see me. She hates him and wants me to hate him too. She's never said that, but I know she does. And besides, I should hate him: he doesn't take care of me or spend time with me. We are poor and he doesn't help us not be poor.

Sometimes I write him a letter back, and sometimes I don't. His letters and questions about my life make me feel happy inside. When his letters come I usually lie in my bed, staring at them for a while. Unlike me, he has very nice handwriting, but beyond that, to know that he has touched this piece of paper with his bare hands, and that this piece of paper was sitting right there in his jail cell with him, and that he wrote on it . . . just for me. It makes me feel kinda, good. Makes me feel . . . almost special.

In his letters from jail he refers to me as Baby Girl. But when he sees me he only calls me that once in a while. I like the way Baby Girl sounds. I wonder what he calls my half-brothers. Sometimes in his letters he sends me pictures of himself. My half-brother Bryan and I sit on my carpeted bedroom floor staring at one of our father's pictures. I stare at the picture even longer than I stared at his letter. During the times when my father's actually out of jail and I see him hanging out in front of my building with all the other men who sell drugs, I can only stare at him for a little while, and when I ask him for money, I usually have my head down.

His pictures allow me to really examine all his body parts, so I can see if they look like mine. I try to figure out if this stranger is really my father.

"Look at his arms; he presses weight like crazy!" Bryan says as he points to the arms on the man they call *our* father. He's wearing a white shirt with no sleeves, dark green jail pants, and sneakers with no laces. He has the straightest face ever, and is standing to the side with his arms crossed over his chest.

I say to Bryan, "His arms are super big and you see them muscles?"

For a quick second, my brain pictures having a daddy like that grab me up and swing me around in his arms as high as he can. I wonder, when he gets out this time if he'll actually be there for me. Will he be one of those dads who come to their children's school concerts? Will he sit down at the dinner table and have dinner with me like the dad on the Cosby Show does? Will he take me to daddy–daughter dances? Will he hold my hand as I cross the road or protect me at night when I'm scared of monsters? Will he do the things daddies do with their daughters, things I don't even know about, because I don't even have a *real* daddy?

"You look like him," Bryan interrupts my thoughts. Secretly I pray Bryan is right. So I stare at the picture, as hard as I can, trying to find features that this stranger might have given me. Maybe if I look like him, I will begin to feel like this stranger is my father. But all I see is that we are both dark skinned with nappy hair.

"You look like him, not me," I say, as if I don't really care. I don't want him to think that I want *our* father to be my dad, or something like that. We both don't like him together. "That's your father," I tease.

"It's yours too," Bryan reminds me before laughing.

"Whatever." I stare at Bryan and try to find something that makes us look alike. I find nothing. I don't look like anyone, not even my mom. My thoughts trail off into an idea that I'm adopted, and one day I'll find my real parents. And we'll be a happy family like people on TV! But then I frown because really . . . it doesn't seem like I'll ever have a father.

* * *

Later that night Mom and I take a cab to Golden Wok, an Asian food restaurant that sits on the corner of Cottage Row and Glen Cove Avenue. The restaurant has lots of Asian decorations around it. Lots of red too, and a clock that looks like a cat; it's cool because the cat's arm waves. The food in this place is okay, but the restaurant always has a different name. We sit in a booth and snack on crunchy strips of fried wontons that I cover with duck sauce.

"Mommy, is duck sauce made of ducks?"

"No. It just tastes good on duck and other things."

"Oh," I say in between mouthfuls of sweet crunchy goodness. I think I'll like duck. I know I like lobster, caviar, chitlins, pigs' feet, clams, scallops and all kinds of other stuff. When we get our food stamps, mom always buys something she calls exotic.

"Give me your order?" I didn't even notice that the waitress was standing here. Mom orders us shrimp eggrolls, shrimp egg foo young, barbeque spare ribs, pork fried rice and two orange sodas.

After the lady walks away, I go back to licking the duck sauce off of my fingers. Our shrimp eggrolls come out quickly and right after I take a bite, Mom says, "So you're father's getting out of jail." Where'd that come from? I think to myself.

I don't really know how I feel about it, so I say, "Oh." Then I find the courage to say, "Mommy, I don't feel like I even know him like that. And he doesn't even know me. I feel like he's a . . . stranger."

Mom doesn't say anything for a while. Then finally she says,

"Shanequa, you were meant to be on this earth. You're gonna do great things in this world, and I know it."

I smile as I cover my eggroll in duck sauce again.

"You know, Shanequa, I was a good student in school. I got good grades, and private schools were looking at me. One school even offered me a scholarship. All my mom would have to pay was one hundred dollars for me to ride the bus during the first year. Then the next year, she wouldn't have to pay anything."

Mom puts her head down and gets silent. After a minute or so, she takes a bite of her eggroll, then says, "Not only was Grammy an alcoholic, but she had five kids. Grammy said, 'How would it have looked if she gave me that much money? What would she do with the other kids?' She said she couldn't afford to take money and food away from them so I could take my ass to some fancy private school!"

I just wanna hug my mommy, and cry for her as she tells me this. I'm scared for her to continue her story because I love my Grammy, but I don't tell her that. The waitress brings us more food, which we cover in duck sauce, before digging in.

Mom looks at me and shakes her head, then says, "After that, I started to give up on my books and started hanging out with the bad crowd." She laughs then says, "That's how I met your damn father."

Her head softly shakes. "Shanequa I was fifteen when I got pregnant with you. I was in the tenth grade." She sighs and shakes her head some more, as if she's laughing at her own self. "Your father was my first." *Yuck! I know what she means.* "I thought he loved me. Well . . . he told me he did. He told me all these wonderful things, and how beautiful and special I was."

"He said that to you, that you were special and beautiful?" I ask her, because there've been many days where I've daydreamed him saying that to me.

"Yes," she answers, then continues, "I believed all of your fathers' bullshit. I was so-o-o young." She shakes her head again. "I let him sweet talk me into taking my virginity." *I scrunch my face up at the thought of the two of them . . . doing it.* "Then when I got pregnant with you, he wanted nothing to do with me anymore." While Mom stares at her food, my heart begins to feel like it hurts and my throat begins to feel like it's swelling.

"He said to me, 'I'm only eighteen and I got two kids already; I can't even take care of them. I don't want any more kids. Get rid of it!" Just when my throat finally had let air pass through it again, the word "it," meaning me, makes my eyes sting from tears I've been fighting to hold back.

"But I didn't care Shanequa; I wanted you!" Thankfully Mom's words help me breathe again. She continues, "Even Grammy told me to get an abortion." Now, I'm saddened even more, but I try to not let her see it as she continues. "Grammy set up the appointment for me to get rid of you. But when I was supposed to go and get it done, my friends and I sat in my room in a small circle on my floor . . . holding hands, and crying."

I try to picture my fifteen-year-old mom sitting with her friends inside of Grammy's house, and me growing inside her belly, and her friends crying about whether or not she should, kill me. I wonder what would have happened if I wasn't born and if she didn't love me so much?

"I just couldn't do it! I wanted to keep you, Shanequa."

I know she means well, but for some reason her words don't make me feel better. It's like I don't even hear them. Mom sips her soda and continues to eat the food that she too has covered in duck sauce.

"Well, I missed my appointment." Mom winks at me. "And when Grammy took me back for another one, I was too far along." I smile a little because that means I was able to be born. But then I think about if that was a good thing or not.

"Shanequa, just do me a favor; wait to have a baby. Wait till you're much, much older! Don't have a baby while you're young like I did. Don't get me wrong, I love you, but if I could do it again," Mom shakes then lowers her head, "I'd wait until I was older, and have you then. It's so hard, to be a teen mother."

Tears form in my mother's eyes and as she lets them fall out, so do I. Then I take a deep breath, and breathe in her smell. My mom's eyes slowly make their way to something on the wall where they become, stuck for what seems like forever. Then finally she says, "You are meant to be on this earth." With her hand on her heart she says, "I know you are. You're special. You were put here on this earth to do something great. I *know* it!" Even though she says it, I still don't feel special. We finish our meal in silence before calling a cab home.

∗ ∗ ∗

A few days later, I'm sitting in my bedroom, listening to the Fat Boys on my new Walkman Mom just got me, when she calls me into the living room because the stranger is here. All of a sudden, I'm nervous. What if he looks at me and remembers that he didn't want me? Will he be mad that I'm still alive?

As I walk into the living room, this tall, dark muscleman greets me with a smile and begins hugging and kissing me. It feels so weird. Mom has never let strangers hug and kiss me like this before. He's really tall. All the people in his family are really tall. But unlike them, he's muscly. I do kind of like his muscles and height; maybe he can protect me from the monsters under my bed.

"So, how have you been?" He has this raspy but friendly sound to his voice, and this look on his face, like he's really interested in what you're saying.

"Good," is all I manage too say. But I really want to ask him, if he wants to be my father now.

"How's school?"

"Okay." He asks me a few more questions to which I give him more one-word answers.

Mom's standing in the kitchen cooking and listening to everything we say. I know she's listening because she keeps making faces to herself whenever he asks me a question.

"Well, Baby Girl, it's time for me to go." His raspy voice ends his ten-minute visit. My heart beats fast because I kind of don't want him to go. Maybe I did something wrong, or maybe I'm boring. Maybe I should have talked to him more; then he would have stayed longer, or even all night.

As I watch him prepare to leave, I try to think of things I can say to him to make him want to stay, but nothing will come into my head or out of my mouth. Instead, I just sit here on our couch, practicing being seen and not heard.

After my father puts his coat on, and has brushed his hairy face against my cheek with his kiss goodbye, he heads for the door. Before he leaves, he turns to me and says, "I'll see you soon, Baby Girl." Then he turns to my mother and says, "Take care. You're doing a good job with her." I wish he would have stayed longer, my brain keeps repeating to me.

When the door closes my mom's screaming begins. "What the fuck was that? He ain't shit!" I keep my mouth closed because I don't know what she wants me to say or do. "He didn't even spend any time with you." She continues and goes on and on about how he ain't shit.

Whatever she was cooking, starts to burn. "Shit!" She yells at the pot as she grabs its handle and yanks it away from the fire. She let's it cool for a second, then stirs whatever it is. Lifting the spoon up to her mouth she tastes the food, "It's just a little scorched." I let out a deep breath I didn't even know I was holding. I hate eating slightly burnt food; it's so gross! This night sucks.

* * *

Mom's wearing her Burger King uniform, and as we sit at our kitchen table eating Whoppers, she gets this weird look on her face. I stare at her with each bite I take.

"Your finger waves look cute; I did my thing with them!" I just smile at her. She's so proud of the hairstyle she gave me. I thought everyone would have liked it too, all of the adults are wearing this style. I don't know how to tell her that girls in the projects are teasing me, and the white kids in school are acting like I'm an exhibit at the museum.

"So you know your father went back to jail, but he's getting out soon."

"Oh yeah?" I raise my eyebrows like I don't care.

"And guess what?"

"What?" I say as my brain struggles to imagine the worst thing possible.

"He'll be staying with us for a while."

My head throws itself back, and my face forms a questioning look. Did she really just say that? She produces a smile that stretches from one ear to the other, and her eyes are shining bright behind her glasses. What a change! I thought she hated him. Seeing her so happy gets me happy too, so I smile back. I smile even harder as I realize I may finally get my Cosby Show family and be able to go to the daddy–daughter dance. He'll probably tuck me in at night too, and protect me from the monsters that sometime live under my bed! Wow this is gonna be great! When I ask Mom for something and she tells me no, I now will have someone else to ask! And it's my very own *daddy*.

Butterflies seem to have flown into my belly when I wasn't looking, but they are flying all around inside my tummy now. I'm scared to ask, because I don't want the wrong answer, but I ask anyway, "Does this mean that you guys are . . ." I take a deep breath, "together?" God, please let her say yes; please let her say yes, God!

She smirks and says, "Something . . . like that."

I'm clapping before the words have completely left her mouth. I can't believe it's really happening to me: I'm gonna have a mommy and a daddy in the same house.

"Maybe you'll have more babies, I want a little sister so-o-o-o-o bad!"

"Relax, Shanequa. You're jumping way ahead of yourself. We are not having a baby. He's just staying here for a while, and we're trying things out." As we continue eating, I let my mind lead me through an imaginary life where I have a little sister, and our parents are married.

* * *

It's the day my father's coming home. In the kitchen, sweet smells capture my attention. I find that Mom has fried pork chops, made cornbread and is beginning to dice potatoes. "I wanna help." I call out over New Edition's "Candy Girl," which my mom is singing loudly to. I'm shocked she hears me.

"I'm making potato salad; you can cut the celery." She grabs them out of the fridge, which has my latest report card taped to it.

"Okay." Mom instructs me on how to dice the celery so they are equally shaped. She's wearing this cute little dress that barely touches her knees. Her boobs are basically falling out it. She has attached a new weave to her hair and it looks kinda cute. Her makeup is done and her lips are bright red. I can't believe it either . . . we're gonna have a man living with us! A man that's *my* father. Hmm, they must be together, if she's doing all this for him. When I'm done cutting the celery, I add it to the bowl of potatoes.

"What do you think my brother will say to me, now that you're with *our* father?" A smile invades my face as I imagine the look that will be on Bryan's face.

She spoons some mayo, mustard and relish into the bowl. "Mix that up." She hands me a big spoon and I start mixing. "Who knows what your brother will say. And who cares." Secretly, I can't wait to tell him; I know he'll be jealous. I know I was when he rubbed it in my face that his mom was boyfriend-and-girlfriend with *our* father. Knowing that I'd never have a real dad felt like a knife went into my heart.

I mix up the potato salad really well before Mom sprinkles garlic powder in it. I mix that in too. "Mom, I'm done." She looks at me with tears running down her face. My heart sinks to my stomach and immediately I am sad for her. Why is she sad though? Is this a trick? Is my father not coming? My heart beats fast as I stare at her face in search of answers. Finally her waist moves away from the counter, and I see the cutting board where she's just peeled and chopped an onion.

"Here, cut these onions." She hands me the knife and wipes her tears with the back side of her hand. As I cut them, I cry too. We add the onions, and a little bit of vinegar, and sugar into the rest of the potato salad. When it's all done, Mom pulls out her yummy deviled eggs and places them on top of it. While my mom continues to sing with the music, I wash my hands, then go back in my room, where I lie on my bed and imagine all kinds of fun daddy-and-daughter moments I'm gonna have. I know my dress will be purple and gold for the daddy–daughter dance. Do they even make purple ties for men? I'm sure he'll want to match me.

After a while I hear a knock on the door. I don't know why my heart just started to pound so hard, but now I feel scared, nervous, happy or something. A few minutes later, Mom says, "Shanequa, come out here and see who it is!"

I can tell she's smiling by the sound of her voice. I take my time walking out there, because what if he's not happy to see me? And what if he hates the idea of living with me and having to take care of me? And why is she acting like it's supposed to be a surprise anyway? When I walk into the living room, I'm shocked to see that he's wearing jeans and a t-shirt. For some reason I thought he'd be wearing jail clothes, not street clothes. Where'd he get 'em from?

"Baby Girl." He picks me up and scoops me into his arms; my cheek brushes his smooth yet hairy face as he plants a kiss onto it.

He carries me over to the couch, where we sit with me on his lap, and him asking me questions that I give one-word answers to. "So how been you doin' in school?"

"Good."

"Umm, okay. You got a best friend?"

"No."

"Umm, well you have friends, don't you?"

"Yes." I want to say, no one wants to be my best friend; they just want to be my friend. I want to tell him how sad I am about that. But why would he care, and what can he do? And besides, I'm not trying to scare him away this time. Since he has agreed to live here, he must really want to be my father; he must not be ashamed anymore that he had me.

As Mom makes our dinner plates, she keeps looking over at us, trying not to miss a word we say. They both seem to be on their best behavior, Mom in the kitchen whipping up something good for her family, Daddy sitting on the sofa with his daughter on his lap discussing her day. "Shanequa, come get your plate," Mom says as she places hers and my father's plates onto the table.

I grab my plate and look around to see where I'm supposed to sit because our table only has two chairs.

"You can eat in your room," Mom says with a smile.

I frown, then walk towards my bedroom door. I sit on my bed, turn the TV on, and eat my food all by myself, while they eat at the table together, having a family dinner . . . without me. I think about going back in there and telling them that I want to eat with them, but then I think that they must not want to eat with me. I guess they wanna talk grown-folk stuff.

It's okay; we'll eat breakfast together tomorrow. Tomorrow . . . we will finally be a complete family!

As I sit on my bed with the door closed, eating the potato salad that I helped make for him, I hear my mother and father sitting at the kitchen table, talking about what my mom has been doing while they weren't together throughout the years. And about some of the women my father has been with when he wasn't locked up. My name . . . only comes up when Mom is talking about how hard it is to raise a child alone, and with little to no money.

As the night goes by, I lie in my bed under the covers, waiting for my father to come into my room and spend time with me and talk to me, to do some of the daddy–daughter things I've been waiting for and dreaming about . . . and then to tuck me in. I can't wait to have him tuck me in *every* night! *This is so crazy; I have a father who lives with me!! What is this gonna feel like? This is just so crazy, I still can't believe it. Me . . . like the white kids in school, will have a father who lives with me!* I grip the covers to hide my smile and the small laughter that has just escaped my lips, just in case my "daddy" walks in, then asks me why I'm smiling.

As the minutes turn into hours, I still just lie here, smiling and waiting for him to at least come and tuck me in. Thoughts about him actually being a daddy to me race through my head over, and over again.

All of a sudden I realize, not only did I just doze off, but it's been almost three hours since dinner, my plate is still on the bottom of my bed, and my father still hasn't come into my room to tuck me in. Now not only am I awake, but I'm really awake and left alone lying in my bed thinking about how wrong Police Officer Cheryl was. She used a really big word when she visited our class that day; she used the word, "rehabilitate." She even had us all pull out our dictionaries to look up the word. After that she told my class that people go to jail to be rehabilitated. But I guess that's not true, because my jailbird father doesn't even know that dads are supposed to tuck their children in at night!

Wouldn't that have been one of the first things they teach all the dads and moms in jail? Especially if they are going to rehabilitate them? When Officer Cheryl described jail, I thought it meant when people do the wrong things, they go to jail and are locked up in a cell like on TV, like when Mr. T from the A-Team got arrested and thrown into jail. But then I thought that if they stayed there for a long time, like most of our dads do in Glen Cove, they'd force them to take classes and stuff, you know, like we do in school. But I thought their classes would be on stuff like what to do when you're a father, or how to do something else in life. I don't know, something like how to cut hair, give people tattoos, become a body builder . . . I don't know. Something else besides selling drugs on the corner and in front of my building where me and my friends live, or something other than how to have a bunch a kids whom they hate and run back to jail to escape from!

But now that I think about it, I've heard my mom and my uncle talk about what jail is really for and what really happens there and why all of our dads keep going back. It's nothing like what Officer Cheryl made it seem. From what I heard my mother and uncle say about it, jail sounds like a place where bad people go when they get too, too bad, like the murderers, rapist, thieves, and drug dealers like my dad. But then when I hear my uncle talking about jail, it sounds like everyone in jail is just hanging out in the cafeteria and sitting with their friends. When it's recess time, all the criminals hang out in the weight room or on the basketball court, trying to have fun while remembering to obey the rules; otherwise they'll be thrown in a box all by themselves for weeks and weeks, until when, I don't know. What I do know is that if I was thrown in a box, I'd come out crazier.

You know what, I think I just answered my own question . . . that's why all our dads aren't scared to go back to jail and be away from their families for a little while. They're having fun hanging with all the bad kids from their school and other people's schools. Jail sounds like a fun place for really bad adults. Maybe that's why when my uncle gets locked up, my family tells my little cousins that he's taking a long, long vacation.

Trying to think about something else, I get out of my bed so I can remind my father that I'm here. Maybe if he sees me, he'll remember that's he's supposed to tuck me in and say goodnight like they taught him in jail, I hope. As I clean up my plate I look around for him and realize he's in the bathroom. When I'm done I just stand there waiting for him to come out. But then Mom tells me it's time for bed, then gives me my hugs and kisses goodnight. I go back in my room put on my nightie, get under my covers and wait for the stranger who we can now call my daddy, to tuck me in.

Shoot! I doze off then have to force myself to wake up. I don't want to be asleep the first time my daddy tucks me in. But again, I doze off. This time when I wake, I check the covers to see if he's been there, but the covers are just as I had left them.

Later that night I'm woken by the gross sounds of the two of them . . . doing it. I turn my TV on really loud so that they'll realize that I'm awake and stop doing . . . it. When they finally fall asleep, I am kept awake by both of them snoring. Again, they are as loud as can be, and this time they sound like they're dying.

In the morning when I wake, my father isn't there.

MOVING ON

Amanda Acevedo

Papi in the Bronx

Amanda Acevedo began this exploration of her father's return to her family in Herstory's Bridges to Justice Workshop in Patchogue, while completing a combined internship with Herstory and Suffolk County's Department of Probation, which allowed her to assist Herstory's founder in working with women and girls writing in Riverhead jail. She took this experience into working intensively with the teen writers among those incarcerated, and now, upon her graduation from Stony Brook University's School of Social Welfare, she is seeking a career that will combine all of her passions. This deeply reflective piece gives testimony to the lack of simple answers in a story of connection and the lack of capacity for connection that the reader will never forget.

August 27, 2002. Ma had just picked up Nana and me from Lala's after spending the weekend with her. It was a beautiful day on the block. At first glance, no one would fathom that corpses had once littered these streets back in the eighties and early nineties—at least that's what Ma told me.

The same cement streets that would hold the makeshift pool my cousins and me would swim in every summer. An inflatable pool intended for private backyards and not in front of an apartment building in the South Bronx; filled by a hose running from my grandmother's kitchen sink, out of her living room window and into the pool.

The block was our playground. The fire hydrants acting as powerful sprinklers in the unbearable summers, illegally opened by someone's uncle with a wrench and often shut down by the local fire department. The buildings that housed my grandmother and younger cousins, but more importantly served as an ideal hide-and-seek location. Unbeknownst to us, its main entrance doubled as an office for drug dealers and their customers, small pieces of white paper discreetly slipped from one palm to another.

In spite of its flaws, I loved the block. The block was home. It was where most of my childhood memories could be traced, this one being my favorite memory to recall.

I remember Nana and me holding on to the *coche* that held my eight-month-old, vibrant, chunky cherub-like baby sister, Ciara, with all of those rolls in her thighs and her tiny bare feet dangling from her stroller, toes spread, without a care in the world.

We were getting ready to make our way down the hill to catch the 17 bus back home when we stopped walking and decided we would not be going home just yet. Someone had told us to come back, so we did as we were told and returned to the front of Lala's building.

We walked the thirty or so feet back to the building and stood there for what I remember to be just a few seconds—or maybe a few minutes? I'm not really sure, I just remember there being a bunch of cars parked up and down the block and kids playing in front of the buildings.

"Why are we back?" I asked Ma, growing increasingly annoyed with being asked to turn around and not being told why. "How long do we have to wait? What are we waiting for? Is it a surprise?"

I hadn't been expecting any surprises. Had I? It was August. My birthday was the month prior. No holidays in August. No, I wasn't expecting any surprises. Besides, no one had even hinted at it being a surprise. No one had hinted at anything.

But there we were. Staring at Tio's double-parked truck on Ave. St. John. Looking back now, that truck held the biggest surprise of my young eleven-year-old life. Then the furthest thing from my mind at the time occurred. The back door of the truck opened and out stepped Papi.

The first thing I spotted was that big cheesy smile he always did. Mouth open. Teeth showing. But only up about to his first molar;

after that his grin was a toothless one. His small light brown eyes, which had always appeared difficult to keep open because they were so small, were the biggest I had ever seen them.

I quickly remembered the last birthday card he had sent me: "This will be your last birthday without Daddy, Princess." I wasn't expecting him so soon! But there he was.

My Papi in the Bronx, not in some remote upstate correctional facility. My Papi all decked out in a red, white and black fitted cap with the sneakers to match, not that swampy green "uniform." My Papi hugging me for as long as we both pleased and not under the watchful eye of a miserable CO.

This hug was just like all the others, except better. The routine dramatic run into his arms and then being lifted above his head, just like he had done so many times before, at the beginning and end of every visit.

What distinguished this hug from all the others was that in that embrace nearly a decade worth of pain had washed away. I wasn't sad that my father had missed my fourth, fifth, sixth, seven, eighth, ninth, tenth and eleventh birthdays. I wasn't upset that he'd never attended any of my school events. My heart was no longer filled with resentment of girls who had the daddy–daughter relationship I could only dream of.

I remember looking at dads pushing strollers or walking their children to school and thinking, *That's strange, dads don't do that,* and quickly reminding myself, *No, my dad doesn't do that.* He can't do that, partly because he's locked up, but if he were home he probably wouldn't do it. Puerto Rican men are raised to NOT cook, to NOT clean and to NOT partake in what they consider maternal activities. Like the time I was a month old and Ma, Papi and I fled to Puerto Rico to stay with my great grandfather because Papi was on the run. Ma had asked him to fix me a bottle and he said he couldn't because he would be yelled at by his grandfather. "That's a woman's job," my great-grandfather would scold.

I was now planning how we were going to make up for lost time and fulfill all the promises Papi had made. Like when he'd place us on his knee in the visiting room and move it up and down really fast and said that when he came home he'd take us horseback riding on *actual* horses. Or when he promised me a trip to Egypt because I was obsessed with mummies, and in his best effort to foster my interest while behind bars he'd sent me books about a little girl close to my age who traveled to Africa.

How long we stood outside and hugged and kissed and reconnected is a blur. The next thing I can remember is me and Nana having a sleepover with Papi. Besides the trailer visit about six years prior, this was the only time we'd done this. We spent the night looking at all the pictures Papi had acquired during his eight-year bid. Reminiscing and being silly. Lala watching, slightly irritated that she wasn't the sole object of her son's affection. Eventually we fell asleep. Nana, Papi and me. Cuddled. In the same bed. For the first time ever.

The following morning I woke up and didn't see Papi in the bed. Nana was there, but he wasn't. Where did he go?

I got out of bed and walked to the living room and there he was sitting on the couch talking to Lala. I plopped myself on the couch next to him still in complete awe. I remembered a time where my father was in a maximum security prison and our visits consisted of sitting on opposite sides of what resembled a fence with just a small square opening at the bottom. We used that opening to hold hands and to pass him nasty frozen hamburgers or wings that had been warmed in a microwave with the remnants of other jailhouse delicacies encrusted on them. But now, now we were sitting side by side on my grandmother's love seat.

The first thing Papi said was how terribly Nana and I slept. How we had kicked him the entire night, forcing him to wake up early. He wasn't complaining though. Believe it or not, I'm convinced he enjoyed being kicked by us.

I giggled at Papi's comment. It wasn't the first time someone had complained about mine or my sister's sleeping. In fact, we'd often been told we inherited that from him.

* * *

Unfortunately that daddy–daughter relationship I spent much of my adolescence dreaming of was just that—a dream, an unrealistic fantasy.

Me being the hopeful, always forgiving daughter that I am, it took several years of broken promises, unmet expectations and tears before the heartbreaking realization that my father did not know how to be a father was made.

The process of realization was a difficult one, one that came in phases. The initial phase was one of excitement, joy and denial. I was happy because my father was home and because he did take my sister and me out.

Like the time we spent my twelfth birthday at Six Flags. And right before that he had taken me shopping for my birthday outfit—a blue T-shirt with a picture of Bob Marley in the center, jean shorts and matching blue Nike Dunks.

"You like these Amanda?"

"Yea Pa."

"Yea, you're right, these are fly!"

He'd been home for about a year now, but being locked up for eight years had left him out of touch with what was in. Often he would ask for my approval on clothing more than once, to make sure it was *fly*.

Although things were good during this time because Papi was a present father and he had money to take us out, there were times that he disappointed me, but I did not fret. He was my Papi; he took us out when he could; I could cut him some slack when he didn't.

I entered the second phase of my realization after my father had been home for about two-three years. Whatever money he had when he first came home had run out. He was no longer taking us out to fun places. Which was fine, one cannot expect to always go out; however, now he wasn't seeing us at all. And that began to bother me. I mean really bother me. I was the only one initiating contact; if I didn't call my father there was a good chance I would not hear from him for weeks, months even.

It was so upsetting! I could not understand how he could stand to stay away from us for so long after not being in our lives for EIGHT YEARS.

What I didn't realize then was that my father did not know how to just be with us, without taking us out. He didn't understand that we wanted to spend quality time with him. That I'd choose a day at home watching crime documentaries and hearing his own personal insider stories of being incarcerated with famous criminals rather than going out shopping.

My personal favorite is when my father told me about the preppy killer, Robert Chambers, a man charged with manslaughter after killing an eighteen-year-old in Central Park during rough sex, allegedly. Papi had done business with this man! He arranged for my mother to meet up with Chambers' wife and exchange some not-so-legal merchandise.

Stories like these intrigued me! For as long as I can remember, I have had almost an unhealthy obsession with everything criminal justice–related. Whether or not my father's incarceration played a role is unknown.

What I do know is that the inconsistent communication made it impossible for me to hear more of my father's stories. Contacting him had become an emotionally draining thing. One that I dreaded because it always ended the same way, me in tears, hanging up knowing that he did not fully comprehend how I was feeling, knowing that there was a good possibility he would not be the first to call me next time, but secretly hoping that he would.

The final phase of my realization came in the form of acceptance. I don't know for sure what triggered this new outlook; I just know that one day it occurred to me that my father was incapable of changing.

And this wasn't an excuse for him. I wasn't saying that he was a victim because he didn't have a father and led a troubled life and therefore I needed to accept him for the way he was—something his family had done for a great portion of his life.

Instead this acceptance was for my OWN peace of mind. I had to tell myself that MY father was not a father. I had to free myself of all expectations and in turn be freed of all potential disappointments.

I like to think that this last phase was a one-time occurrence, like taking a band-aid off. The band-aid's off and you no longer have to anticipate the pain associated with taking it off. But that wasn't the case. I had accepted, but there were still times that I was hurt and upset by the lack of paternal instinct that my father possessed.

✳ ✳ ✳

"Have you ever thought about seeing a therapist?"

There was a brief pause in our conversation after my best friend asked me this.

Hundreds of miles away in California, Breante could sense how much my most recent conversation with my father was bugging me.

Damn it! I had kept telling myself that I was done being upset over his not being a father.

Boy was I wrong.

"You know, I've actually never considered it until now," I responded to Breante after a few awkward seconds of him staring at me blankly over my computer screen.

Earlier that day my father had sent me a text message. "Hey big girl, how's it going?" he asked.

"Pretty good U?" I responded, keeping my text as short as possible, while not being rude.

Three minutes later I received a text I had not been anticipating.

"I'm good, thank you. Anything new, when do you graduate?"

Ugh. He's asking me when I graduate. WHY? He wasn't worried about my graduation those months he hadn't contacted me.

A couple weeks prior I had decided I would not be inviting my father to my graduation. Looking back on the last two years of my graduate program I could not identify one time in which he had been helpful in my acquiring this degree.

Instead what came to mind were the countless times my mother's boyfriend had come to the rescue when I was carless and unable to make it to school or internship, the several thought-provoking conversations about social injustice he and I had shared, him the son of a social worker, my future profession.

Shaun was golden, and for that I had decided he would receive my fourth and final graduation ticket, him along with my mom and two younger sisters; I couldn't think of four better people to share my special day with.

I had it all figured out until my father poked his head back into my life; that one text was the catalyst for the emotional tsunami that was about to come.

A tsunami because of the overwhelming feeling of sadness, disappointment and uncertainty that overcame me after he asked, "Am I going to be able to go to your graduation?"

So sure and adamant about him not being there just days ago, I began to question my decision.

Why was I questioning myself? This was his doing.

Disappointed in my relationship with my father, that it had even come to this, I questioned whether he was worthy or not of attending my big day.

Tsunami—also appropriate considering the immediate onset of tears and having to run to my job's bathroom. I couldn't believe that he had still had this effect on me!

The deeper reason behind the tears was hard to place. I was upset with him, but I was also sad. I wanted him there, but he had made it so that he was not welcome.

"I already picked the people that I would like to be there," I finally responded, imagining how he must've felt when he read that. How crushed he had to be, knowing that his first born would be receiving her Master's Degree and he would not be there to witness it only hurt ME more.

All he said was "I understand."

That was it. There was no fight. He didn't try to convince me to invite him. He didn't tell me how much it would mean for him to be there. He didn't fight for me, and his passivity infuriated me.

He didn't understand. He didn't understand I was hurting as a result of telling him that he was not invited. That I was hiding in a bathroom, splashing water on my face in a weak attempt to conceal my red, puffy, wet eyes. He didn't understand that I wanted him there.

"I wish you would've shown more interest. It really hurts me that you don't."

I put aside my tough act and for the first time in a long time I was vulnerable with my Papi. However, that was short lived after my father wished me the best, told me I was special and that he loved me—a response that came naturally to him, not because he didn't care about me and want a better relationship, but because he did not know how to initiate a healing process and had proven in the past to fear my rejection.

Knowing this did not stop me from telling him how I REALLY felt.

"It's always 'You are special, Amanda.' Or 'God bless you, Amanda.' It's never 'What can I do to fix it, Amanda?' I hate that your absence bothers me as much as it does. The biggest mistake you made was to allow another man to do for your kids what YOU should have been doing."

I wanted that one to sting.

"You're not the first person I think to call when I have an issue because you have NEVER given me reason to believe you're reliable.

For this graduation I have chosen to invite people who have contributed to me and my success in a positive way."

And even with all that I could not maintain my hard front. It was just that, a front.

"It breaks my freaking heart to look back on these past two years and know that there's no positive memory with you attached to it.

This is by no means to disrespect you but to let you know if I know heartbreak it is because of you. Time and time again. Something you've never failed at Pa."

Katherine De la Cruz

The Longest Wait of My Life

Katherine was part of Herstory's "Our Story" workshop, which engaged 450 Educational Opportunity Program students at Stony Brook University over the course of three summers, as part of their required freshman orientation. Working to incorporate Herstory's "dare to care" technique as they wrote to contribute to a movement for civil rights and economic justice, these entering students explored ways in which their own stories might dare current and future decision makers in the larger community to care.

As Katherine explored the technique, adding a new scene each week, she was able to provide her classmates not only a riveting picture of a three-year-old watching an unimaginable crime, but of the way in which having a parent in prison casts a continual shadow of sorrow and "otherness" over the lives of children left behind. The response of her classmates, as they showed her how she had allowed them to walk in her shoes, helped break that isolation as it strengthened her resolve to use her story to help others. This selection is reprinted from *VOICES: Memoirs from Herstory inside Long Island's Correctional Facilities,* published in 2012, a book that has been used to train incoming correctional officers and is used as a text by criminology classes in several Long Island Colleges.

I find myself on this huge bus, sitting next to complete strangers and somehow still feeling like I have something in common with each and every one of them. Looking around while I'm on an overnight bus ride, which feels like the longest ride of my life, I see people who look just as exhausted and anxious as me. At last, as the sun is rising, while I stare out the window, I've arrived at this destination that at this point is still unfamiliar to me, but I'm looking around trying to guess. All I see is a building made of brick with a fence as long as a football field surrounding the entire thing and what looks like barbwire at the top of it. The feeling of separation and coldness as I enter the building is something inevitable. As I walk in, there are a number of men and seldom women in uniform awaiting my arrival. After I go through all security measures I am finally allowed in. I go sit at a table and take another look around, staring at all the unfamiliar people I sat right next to on the bus ride here. I stop moving my eyeballs from left to right and fixate them on one target, a door in which the people that walk out are the only ones that can walk back in. This feels like the longest wait of my life and perhaps it feels that way because I have waited all my life for this moment.

A man finally exits out of the door and I automatically recognize everything about him—from the way he walks, to the form of his facial features and even his voice. He sits right across from me, only to stare and await some type of dialogue to form. I don't know where to start or even how to start; it is like sitting by a stranger.

No one would have guessed this man to be my birth father. I'm sixteen years old at this point, and finally it hits me that my father is a stranger to me. As I say "hello" and call him by his real name instead of "Dad," I keep having flashbacks of the very moment where everything changed, the reason for my visit and the reason for him being in this place.

My memories of my father are for the most part nonexistent; I spent the majority of my childhood pretending I wasn't as affected as I really was by his lack of involvement. And the rest of my life I spent making up excuses for both my father and mother. My mother and father formed an unusual couple. They never really looked happy together, just content, and eventually you would look at them and realize they were both just putting up with one another. Through them I learned to put up. That's what got me sitting in this room, staring at my father through this transparent glass, which separated his world and mine. His world filled with limitations and my world of limitless possibilities. I found myself even beyond the resentfulness, wanting to share a portion of my freedom with him. For as long as I could remember it had been that way. It had been years and I had begun to stop missing him, perhaps he had been gone so long that I had become accustomed to living the life I was living without him.

He proceeded to ask me how I'd been, but I couldn't help thinking to myself, Is he just asking to start a conversation? Perhaps he actually was interested in what had happened in the last thirteen years of my life at this point. So in a courteous manner I answered that I had been good, although you can only imagine what I was really thinking. After staring at each other in complete silence the guard warned us that we must begin to say our goodbyes and although I couldn't say a word, I watched my father disappear into the very door he came out of. I sat in this wooden jail chair and stared at the emptiness that just a few moments before had been his presence. As the tears ran down my face like a waterfall, I placed my hand on the glass and whispered into the emptiness, "I forgive you, Dad."

✳ ✳ ✳

As I walked out of the prison where my father had been all my childhood, I shed some more tears and mounted back on the bus awaiting the long awkward bus ride back once again. But this time on my ride back I had a lot of reflecting to do. Somehow, although this long ride wasn't new to me, I still couldn't adjust to it all. Finally, after fifteen minutes of waiting, the bus pulled away from the same building whose picture was still engraved into my mind.

As I proceeded to put headphones in my ears and tried to ignore the noise of these unknown people, I pressed PLAY on the purple iPod my mother had given me. As I listened to the music, I closed my eyes and tried to get to a tranquil zone where nothing and no one could bother me. After ten minutes I finally achieved the level of relaxation I had aimed for, only to have the calm broken by my thoughts. My favorite song had come on and with every high pitch and change of beat, the scene faded more and more, until it completely disappeared. I can't speak for anyone, but it's the worst feeling ever, avoiding remembering certain things but then having the very thing you're avoiding come up time and time again. It's like

I can feel it now—the harder the sound of the drum, the more it hurt to think. I finally just let the feeling take over me and closed my eyes, envisioning a scene that was so specific and crucial to my life.

$$* * *$$

There she was, a young girl of at least three years of age, sitting on this brown and tan striped couch with her aunt, watching a popular Spanish show on a Spanish network which was quite popular where she came from. As the girl looks at her aunt she can't help but smile. Her aunt was glowing and her laughter could fill every corner of her eighteen-floor apartment building with sound. The young girl proceeded to the kitchen, which was down this long, narrow, dark hallway right by the main entrance to the apartment. I couldn't help but giggle at the image of the three-year-old girl, shorter than the table she was standing in front of, yet still completely filled with enthusiasm as she attempts to fill this big aluminum cup, which is her aunt's favorite, with ice tea. Before she could finish a man walked in. I could at this point describe every last aspect of him, as though I were being questioned by a police officer. He looked about six feet tall in my vision, with a navy blue sweater with a hood which covered his face and protected his identity from me. He just had walked in, didn't look anywhere besides forward, and proceeded to the living room. The young girl with terror reading all over her face stayed underneath the table. In her face you could also tell she sensed danger and from her vantage point all she could hear was six loud thumps, but it was louder than a nail to a hammer or the sound of a hammer falling to the ground.

When I began to hear these sounds within my vision, the music became louder, and it finally drove me to remove the earphones. But even after that the sound wouldn't stop. I searched deep within the vision again and replayed that very moment, and after the second time I could finally depict the sound. The man exited quickly following the noise. The young girl attempted to call her aunt's name from the kitchen and be sure she was okay, but all she heard in response was silence. The very thing that scared her at that point was the silence. So the girl ran to the living room as if she sensed something was wrong, and there it was, as sure as she said it—her aunt's body on the striped couches—but this time they were colored tan, brown and stains of red. The television and the show still on, she could hear someone's voice coming from the phone and just a body lying lifeless there.

She looked so helpless and confused, so she picked up the phone and heard a woman say, "Hello," with a voice that was too similar to that of her mother's. And sure enough it was the young girl's aunt's sister, and in an ironic shift of events, also the girl's mother.

* * *

When I realized the vision was now over, I wiped these tears that ran down my face, because I could relate to this girl as if I were living her life. This vision came to me after I visited my father in prison and I remembered just the things that happened throughout my life and how one day I was that young girl. That young girl was still inside me and the man I had just sat in front of, staring through the translucent glass, was her father, my father, our father. He was the man in my vision and the cause for everything I stood for at this point. I was that little girl who had witnessed it all.

The next thing I remember clearly was sitting in a room with the sadness and disturbing memory of my aunt lying on the couch. I remember feeling overwhelmed as I observed police officers run in and detectives taking photographs of the crime scene. I remember the police asking everyone questions and I just sat and heard all they had to say. I had the answers to their questions and couldn't communicate myself with them. Perhaps it was because I was three and no one expected me to know. But that moment was the moment in which I grew up.

* * *

I know you hear your whole life the world say that you don't know any better when you're three, but I had broken that stereotype. Better yet, my situation had broken that stereotype—not many girls go through traumatic experiences like that. My family had never agreed on much of anything except the fact that any girl who had ever witnessed that needed help. So my mother thought I should give it a try and honestly what better could I do but go to some psychologist.

Knowing then what I know now I wouldn't have gone, but I was three and all I could do was obey what my mom told me to do. So that's when it all started that my father, although he had been gone all my life, was the centerpiece around every last thing I did. I only had attended two sessions of this counseling and already I thought to myself this is pointless, because no matter what, no one could take me out of that moment. It's a moment that I would carry in my memory and chest for the rest of my living days here on this earth.

I can remember sitting in the living rooms of my family members' houses and hearing them talk about the situation as if they even lived it. I think they just didn't consider my feelings because I was three. I couldn't believe how selfish they all were and it hurt me to think that they couldn't see my hurt. I spent so much time in these counseling sessions, each one getting more pointless than the one before. When were these people going to get that I wasn't crying because I couldn't anymore, and that I was honestly going to be okay? I didn't want anyone to baby me. I wanted to live my life normally without having the world feel bad for me.

* * *

In middle school I was still taking counseling sessions and I hated to tell people that, so not even my closest friends knew. I built my life around the idea that friends didn't exist and best friends aren't true friends, so I never felt left out. Around school you'd see everyone with someone else and I was always alone. Some of my best times of the day were when I could just be alone. I would try to convince the world friends don't exist and now thinking about it, maybe I was jealous that everyone had someone to talk to and I didn't. I spent so much time trying to isolate myself from the world so no one would find out about my life or what had happened to me. And this idea worked for a while, but there were times I was fed up and I'd sit in a bathroom stall in my gym locker room and just cry. I never liked to show people my emotions and somehow I couldn't help but burst out into tears.

Graduating from middle school marked the end of my counseling. You see my mother had given me the choice to stop going, so I did. The end of this very memory took me right back to the scenery

I was passing on my way home, the cars zooming past us and the emptiness that submerged my existence.

Here I was on this bus thinking about every minute memory I had that built up to this memory. The more I thought the more I realized that the pictures of these memories remain instilled in my mind and the image is ever so clear. My father, although he had committed wrongful actions, always taught us to never lie or cheat and above all, even though he did wrong that day, he was a man of his word. I can still place myself in the moment, the hour, the minute, the very second in which he gave himself in to the authorities.

It was the very next day after it all had happened. I watched out of my sixth-floor apartment window as my father strolled up the hill in my neighborhood park in hand cuffs with two men in uniform escorting him. I remember waving goodbye, but not realizing what that goodbye signified. I had said bye many times before as he walked up that same hill, but I always knew he'd return, but in my heart I knew this time was different.

That hill brought back the few memories I had of my father to me. I had fallen and scraped my knees there numerous times before, so many times I had lost count. My father loved taking me to that park and chasing me around trying to teach me to ride a tricycle. As I watched tears of desperation and sorrow run down my mother's face, all I could do was hug her and hold on tight. Little did I know it'd be the last time we hugged that significantly.

✳ ✳ ✳

At the beginning my mother spoke to no one about what had happened with my father. She stayed home and cried most of the time and I couldn't take it, I found myself wanting to alleviate her problems. It was like an emotional cut, something I couldn't put a bandage over and just leave all alone because I knew it wouldn't heal any quicker. My childhood was spent trying to relieve the pain my mother felt, knowing what my father had done and attempting to forget and help her forget. At times I felt like the adult, and it was sickening to me. I had no time for anything—all I could do was sit and think of ways to make my mother happy. So I started off doing small things for her. I would sweep and mop and even wash dishes.

And as the years progressed I started realizing the damage I had done to both my mom and myself. I let her become too accustomed to always having me around, and now it was really hitting me. As the years progressed, I continued doing all those things, but now added cooking and doing laundry to that list—basically I was doing all the things mothers are supposed to do. My mother and I never had one of those relationships where we spoke about things, or even hugged. It was one of those relationships where you love someone from afar and that's what I was doing watching her and loving her but yet never letting her know. I would never admit this to her, but I spent a lot of time feeling guilty like in some way me and my brother were at fault for my father's actions. I never asked her, but I always felt below everyone at home, and it wasn't until I got older that I began to question myself. I would think to myself, What am I doing wrong? And the answer was, Nothing.

My mother, her whole life, had problems with love and relationships and somehow after every heartbreak and breakup I found myself trying to pick up the broken pieces and put them back together. It was my fault, I'd say to myself to make me feel better, although inside I always felt like the person being taken advantage of. I was the true victim, but still I acted as though nothing bothered me and instead made sure that my mother was okay. Throughout the first couple of months of my father's imprisonment my mother faithfully would go visit him and then have me and my brother visit him too. When she finally decided she couldn't handle this relationship from the two different worlds they were in, she suddenly stopped and I started to break down inside at this point.

I never knew what it meant to me for my parents to be together but at all costs, even if they would be at each other's throats all the time, I wanted them to be together. I continued visiting my father along with my brother and that's what got me on this bus. But just as my mother did, my brother stopped coming to see him.

The first time I remember actually coming in to the jail and visiting him I was still so young, I was only six-years-old and still I felt more mature than ever. You had to have heart to enter these places and leave them the same. As I sit and remember the very first time I saw him in an all navy blue uniform, I guess it's hard to forget. I took a picture of him and it lies on the nightstand right by my bed. As I still spend my weekends cleaning my house, just as I did before. I often come across it and I dust it off and stare at it for a while. I swear it's like the more I look at it, the clearer I remember it all.

Walking through the lie detector and feeling as if they had stripped me completely naked, but I still had clothes on, that feeling of discomfort was inevitable. You can only imagine the way I felt when I had to keep reliving it. It was as if I had tripped and fallen one day and had to constantly relive the moment. It was painful and I for one couldn't take it anymore. Walking in and anticipating my father's walk to the empty table at which I sat and conversing for a few moments knowing that in an hour I would be back on that bus.

No matter how much I tried to get my mind set on how things were going to be, as I approached the exit of the jail, I always suddenly turned back to look and see if my father had come behind me and we would leave together but it never happened. Silly me thinking I could change the course of time or the events that occurred just because I was unhappy. I was selfish, but I had every reason to be in my eyes—my mother was selfish, and my father perhaps the most selfish of us all, and together they taught me to be selfish. He never really spoke much on the subject and I honestly never felt the need to bring it up, but his repeated I'm-sorry's told it all. I didn't see myself ever getting past the moment and ultimately that affected my relationship with my mother.

I never understood her, as she never understood me, and perhaps that was my fault. I never tried hard enough to get close to her, because I felt somehow that by helping her with all the things that worried her I was doing her a favor. I never realized just how important it would have been for my mother and me to discuss my father's actions and for me to express to her the guilt I felt, because I thought she blamed me for all the things that went wrong in her life. My mother grew accustomed to life with me helping her fixate on all the little issues that would bother her. When my twin brother and sister were now born, I should have known things weren't going to change. Once again I found myself fixing one more of my mother's issues. When it wasn't housework, it became her relationship issues, and now to add to all that was already on my shoulders, I had a baby brother and sister here.

* * *

My mother worked hard to maintain us living the life my father had accustomed us to live. She worked in this hospital right up the hill from my apartment building. It was located right up the same hill in which I had viewed my father walk up handcuffed. I couldn't help it that every time I walked up the hill I felt like I was losing a part of me. In many ways I still felt my father very much a part of me. I found myself always comparing how life would have been with him around. I found him to be my inspiration because I knew although I loved him dearly that I didn't want to be anything like him and that motivated me in school. My mother was never too concerned with grades because she grew complacent with the low grades my brother and sister brought home.

I remember the day I spent a whole two weeks on a paper and got an A+. I ran home to show my mom as she was watching her favorite Spanish soap opera, but I missed the opportunity in between her hold-on's and give me a second's. It finally turned into that she fell asleep once more. I started honestly, believing it didn't matter to her so if she wouldn't ask I wouldn't tell. Maybe it was because my mom received an eighth grade education and she somehow was always jealous of all the things I had accomplished and she wasn't able to. My mother knew I was capable and wanted the same for my brother and sister, but they were their own persons and my mother couldn't see past all that.

It started off with small things—honors assemblies, report cards, unviewed test scores and quickly before I knew it. It was my senior year in high school and she was doing the same thing she always did. I learned to fend for myself very early in life. So for anything that had to do with being accepted to college or even scholarships I had worked my hardest to win, she never showed up. After a while I gave up, lost interest in doing almost everything, just because I knew it didn't matter to anyone.

* * *

A decade later I'm on my way, embarking on one of the greatest moments of my life; I remember the butterflies in my stomach as I began to zip up this white gown that concealed the white dress and shoes I was wearing. I remember clearly walking down this long narrow pathway, standing next to all these people that were familiar to me at this point, but sooner or later I would forget all about. The moment was coming and I could feel it as I got closer and closer to the podium. It was a moment of anxiety, which I couldn't remove myself from, it was just another thing that was out of my control.

As the stage got closer, all the people who at one point seemed minute, enlarged right before my eyes and a sense of relief took over me. All I could think about wasn't what I was going to say, but the estranged relationship I had with my father and the nonexistent relationship between my mom and me.

I approached the stairs that led to the podium and I lifted a side of this big all-white gown I had on, afraid I might trip. There I was— all these words written on paper and somehow not finding a way to communicate them through my shaky hands and low voice. It was this very moment that put me in the same situation I had been in, staring at my father through that translucent glass. Somehow I always find that happens to me when I get nervous. I began with "Good afternoon, Ladies and Gentlemen and most importantly my fellow class of 2010." After saying this I began to choke up on the stage, remembering all the amazing small moments that led to this everlasting lifelong memory.

I went into high school thinking I just want to do enough to get by. By my tenth-grade year I decided I'm going to do all I can to do better then everyone around me, but in 11th grade I realized I have to do enough to make myself proud and not only do better than the people who are at my level but somehow surpass their intellect, because at this point I realized the world was my competition. Better yet, my whole life I felt was an ongoing war with the world. I wasn't sure when it was time to just let everything go. Whenever I got up, I felt like the world would dig me in deeper and I began to be inspired to rise above it all.

I remember this feeling I felt at this point. I wasn't addressing my classmates as valedictorian or even salutatorian—I had accomplished what any person with leadership qualities would of loved—I had been president of the student body at my school. I know the position sounds mediocre, but being in this environment was the only time I didn't think of what I had been through all my life. I continued addressing the graduating class, telling them how proud I was of being able to say I knew each and every one of them. I always saw myself standing right in the position I was in right this second. I just didn't see the day coming soon enough. But I knew what it was going to take to get me there. I was at this point where I had become my own mom and dad and I never once let my father's absence affect where I was going in life. My constant reliving of it every time I took a step onto that bus drove me to a sea of tears in which I was constantly swimming.

Years later here I am, no longer taking those long pointless trips to the middle of nowhere to visit a stranger. Instead I'm in the place I call my home, awaiting the phone call that never happens and the letters I never receive. I give up, I say. I forgive him, I can finally say, because I grew out of the grudge against him. I'm different, I can yell, because he's my inspiration for what I don't want to become. I am who I am because I created all the parts that compose me! And I live for me, because if I don't, no one else will!

REFLECTIONS

Rachel Wiener

A REFLECTION

 This project would never have existed without Rachel Wiener, who for over twenty years has been social worker, mentor and mother to the young people of Central Islip High School who have needed her the most. As part of the school's Center for Peace, her caring goes far beyond the walls of her first-floor office and the hours of the school day. She has played an important role in seeing every high school writer in this collection through challenging life moments, be they the birth of a first baby, the loss of a stable home, the sudden coming of new information about a parent's sentence in prison, or the homecoming of a parent with all the joys and challenges that this brings.

One of the highlights of my career as a high school social worker is to have been part of the Herstory Youth Writing for Justice Program for the past two years. Being part of the process of watching these wonderful students share their pain and sadness, their hopes and dreams, has been a wonder to witness. Although it is probably the first time these students have had someone listen and truly hear them, it is a gift for both the teller and the listener.

I have to believe that along with this power of the word, there can be continued action, especially with those people whose needs are so obvious: the need to have someone truly care. For many students school is their safe place, a haven where there are people who acknowledge them, friends to socialize with and food to eat. They may be failing classes, but they crave the stability and routine that a school schedule offers. Whereas vacations allow many of us to travel, relax at home and unwind, for many it means days alone in their room or on the streets with nothing to do, little or no food to eat and few people around to care for them. It is so important that anyone who works in a school realize that each student has a story to tell, which needs to be heard. The student who falls asleep in class, who comes to school in dirty clothes, who has no friends, who is the class clown, who asks to leave the room; there is a story that if allowed to be heard will most certainly flourish.

Tanasha, with her story of abandonment, abuse and distrust, when given the permission to write the words, could no longer hold them in and gifted us with her prolific, beautifully worded and emotionally draining history, Malaysia's moving story of the loss of growing up with her father and her dreams and hopes for a reunion that might not come true anytime soon, Nicole poetically bringing us into her search for her real father and finding along the way that she cares about all three of the candidates, Antisha, who after years of dreaming about her father's release from jail, painfully realizes that her expectations might not come to fruition, Desmond, who suffered being bullied as a child, relating a disturbing confrontation with police in which his brother is arrested, Destiny so eloquently relating the stories of her youth, including the loss of innocence, and lastly, Aysha writing so uniquely about losing her parents to drugs and jail and still being able to succeed in her goals.

These adolescents who decided they could trust me to protect them from harm when agreeing to allow not only myself, but Erika, Serena and Barbara to listen in a safe space, helping them to release their demons. For them the risks were many; for me it changed my life, and I thank them with all my heart for believing in the process and for taking the risk.

I am retiring at the end of this school year. I lie awake thinking about how I feel about leaving my job as a high school social worker. It is both happy and sad. Sadness fills my heart when I think of all I am leaving behind. Constant thoughts enter my mind, keeping me from sleep, filling me with worry and as I realize I am not only leaving a place, but a life. Twenty or so years of stories—many told, some held back—causing me to make them up in my mind. I feel compelled to watch the local news or search the newspapers, hoping not to see another one of our youth hurt or in trouble. Students visit, send pictures, call to tell me how their lives are going. Happy tales and heartbreaking sadness. It is hard to leave it behind. Can one ever forget the faces, the tears, the laughter, the stories? I know I won't be able to—nor do I want to. They have become part of me, allowed me to stare fear in the face and will it to be gone, both for others and for me. It can't help but wear one down, but how wonderful a ride it has been. I cry over those that I will not meet, fear that those students who need me might not get the care they so deserve. Selfish thoughts, but I can't help but think them.

I will always remember Herstory, the power of words, the gifted students who so beautifully wrote about growing up affected by the penal system, and their hopes and dreams.

Barbara Allan

A REFLECTION

There is something deeply humbling about the rare person who, even after forty years of changing thousands of lives, will say, "I merely responded to what I saw," rather than "I created this." Now in her late seventies, Barbara travels all over the state, giving presentations on the needs of prison families and talking to students and legislators, but mostly making herself available night and day for the calls that will come from people who suddenly find themselves with a loved one in prison or a loved one just getting out. But she keeps a special place in her heart and her week for the young writers of Central Islip High School.

When someone you love has been arrested, a feeling of helplessness and panic sets in. Society often accuses, ostracizes, and sentences a family member at the same time as the offender. The family feels ashamed, embarrassed and stigmatized. Often the person taken away from the family is the sole provider. Everything around you seems to be falling apart. If you are an adult, you need to apply all the coping mechanisms you have developed throughout your lifetime.

If you are a child and are affected by this traumatic, life-changing event, you do not have the internal resources to know how to survive, so you look to the adults in your life to take the lead.

While the caregiver is trying to deal with his or her own reality, the children are often left to find their own way. Too often, when a parent leaves, the children think that they must have done something wrong to cause this emptiness.

When a mother is sent to jail, there might not be a family member or friend to help pick up the pieces, leaving the child to be thrust into the foster system.

The children who are left behind feel that they have no voice. No one is listening to their pain. Often they suffer indignities at the hands of those who are designated to protect them.

I am the co-founder of Prison Families Anonymous, an organization that is in existence to offer information, hope and advocacy to those who are affected by the criminal justice system. I learned the intricacies of the system first hand when my husband was arrested and my children were denied access to their father.

My husband murdered his father during an alcoholic blackout. He had been diagnosed manic depressive and was under the care of a psychiatrist. In my naiveté, I expected him to be sent to a treatment facility. He instead was sentenced to "hard labor" at a maximum security prison.

How do I navigate the system? It would be a lonely journey. I knew that I did not have the wherewithal to find the answers. There were so few resources in the community that I found myself isolated. The only comfort that I could find was with others who were walking the walk with me.

Once I discovered that I was going to survive, I determined that, if possible, I would be there for others who were taking this journey. Prison Families Anonymous was the result.

We had weekly support group meetings with wives, parents, and siblings of the incarcerated. Anyone who currently or ever had a loved one in the juvenile or adult criminal justice system was welcome.

As I listened to the stories of the young writers who contributed to this anthology, I thought back to the day my daughter and her peers sent a note to "PFA." In their wisdom, the children banded together and asked why they did not have a group like the grownups. What a revelation! Of course our children were impacted by the absence of a parent, and they too needed a release valve. Their situations were unique and they felt the loss and the stigma. With no other outlet, they instinctively bonded with each other.

We listened to our children and we created a prison families children's group

Forty years have passed and now we are reading the stories of a new generation of children affected by this era of mass incarceration. The haunting stories of Malaysia, Antisha, Tanasha, Desmond, Nicole, Aysha, Destiny, Shanequa, Amanda and Katherine remind me of why I continue to do this work.

As husbands, wives, sons and daughters returned to their communities, we realized that we needed to offer reentry resources as well. We also realized that when we saw an injustice, we needed to address it. If we who have a vested interest in righting a broken system do not speak out, who will?

In the forty years of our existence we have partnered with many other organizations. In order to make a difference in our own lives and the systems that influence our lives, we need to form an alliance and eradicate the "them" and "us" mentality. (See our list of resources at the end of this volume.)

Serena Liguori

A REFLECTION

Herstory's co-director, Serena Liguori, works tirelessly to ensure that stories created by all writers in Herstory's workshops are given the chance to heard by key decision makers at the heart of family and social justice issues. Her passion for changing broken systems and supporting prison families comes from many years of advocacy for families impacted by incarceration and family violence, including her own.

What is so important about maintaining ties with a parent behind bars? Isn't it better to keep a child away from prison or jail? All children at every age have a deep need to be accepted and loved by their parents. Children want to love their parents despite their parents' inability to be present. Parents shape our perception of the world and have lasting influence on our lives, well beyond childhood. And maybe this love is complex; maybe children of the incarcerated come to know responsibility and the pain of loss much too early in life. And yet, unequivocally, parents play a critical role, whether they are a constant or a figure speckled by absence.

Most people think of prisons and jails as places that house adults, not children. However, children are punished as a result; it is children who become the immediate collateral damage of sentencing doled out by the courts on a parent. They suffer deep and long-lasting wounds, separated from the parents they love. The loss of a parent to prison or jail has the same impact on children as the death of a parent. The struggle to survive this debilitating loss and the larger systemic impact of incarceration is reflected in the passages shared by our young writers. They have shared their souls here every week as they came to the writing workshop, giving us a peek into their lives. These writers have sustained the stigma of incarceration wrongly placed on them because of an incarcerated parent. They have withstood the disdain of blind mainstream society and continue to prove everyone who predicted their failure wrong.

For so many of our writers, coming to terms with the expectations of what role a parent may have in their life after coming home from incarceration is challenging, sometimes even devastating. And yet, what you hear in the voices of the writers here is resilience. Many psychologists do not understand how a child develops resilience, where it really comes from or how it can be predicted. They aren't able to quantify how much resilience a child may or may not have. And yet what I know is that through these writing workshops, through the support of teachers and mentors whom they write alongside, our writers have tapped into hope and empowerment.

What I have seen in countless workshops is children who have survived, with dignity and insight beyond their years, the very worst that life could throw at them. They comfort each other with silent nods and small hugs. They listen to each other's stories and in doing so, incredibly, find ways to survive the loss of a parent to prison or jail. Finding ways to cope with this loss correlates directly to their ability to successfully navigate so many of life's other challenges of adolescence and young adulthood. It is my hope that for all of our writers, the safe space of the workshops will continue to remind them of their deep worth. Children of incarcerated parents are smart, resilient and incredibly strong. These are children with stories to grow us all, stories with bright futures to be had.

Sister Elaine Roulet pioneered the creation of children's visiting rooms in many of the upstate prisons, giving children a fighting chance to create bonds with their mothers.

RESOURCES FOR PRISON FAMILIES

RESOURCES FOR PRISON FAMILIES

PRISON FAMILIES ANONYMOUS
Telephone: 631-943-0441
Address: Sarisohn Law Building, 350 Veteran's Memorial Highway, Commack, NY 11725
Web site: www.pfa-li.com

STATE PROGRAMS

Big Brothers, Big Sisters
Check your state for available resources and programs.

SKIP, Inc. Community Resource Services
Check your state for available resources and programs.

ARIZONA

MentorKids USA
Telephone: 480-767-6707
Address: 8960 E Raintree Drive, Suite 300, Scottsdale, AZ 85260
E-mail: info@mentorkidsusa.org
Web site: www.mentorkidsusa.org

Middle Ground Prison Reform
Telephone: 480-966-8116
Address: 139 East Encanto Drive, Tempe, AZ 85281-6624
E-mail: middlegroundprisonreform@msn.com
Web site: http://www.middlegroundprisonreform.org/

ARKANSAS

Club Buddies—BECOME A STAR
  Telephone: 479-273-7187
  Address: P.O. Box 448, Bentonville, AR 72712
  E-mail: sabrina.rampy@cox-internet.com
  Web site: www.bgcbentoncounty.org

HIP Mentoring Program.
  Telephone: 870-773-4655
  Address: 2904 Arkansas Boulevard, Texarkana, AR 71854
  E-mail: mschroeder@swacmhc.com

BALTIMORE

U.S Dream Academy
  Telephone: 410-772-7143
  Address: 10400 Little Patuxent Parkway, Suite 300, Columbia, MD
    21044
  E-mail: info@usdreamacademy.org
  Web site: www.usdreamacademy.org

CALIFORNIA

Families and Criminal Justice
  Address: Box 50-683, Los Angeles, CA 90050
  E-mail: WritetoFCJ@hotmail.com
  Web site: www.familiesandcriminaljustice.org

Centerforce
  Telephone: 415-456-9980
  Address: 2955 Kerner Blvd., 2nd floor, San Rafael, CA 94901
  E-mail: cburton@centerforce.org
  Web site: www.centerforce.org

Community Mentoring Connections
  Telephone: 209-533-1397, ext. 229
  Address: 427 N. Highway 49, Suite 305, Sonora, CA 95370
  E-mail: elinehan@atcaa.org
  Web site: atcaa.org

Project AVARY
  Telephone: 415-382-8799
  Address: 385 Bel Marin Keys, Suite G, Novato, CA 94949
  E-mail: info@projectavary.org
  Web site: www.projectavary.org

Start with a Story
  Telephone: 510-745-1511
  Address: 2450 Stevenson Boulevard, Freemont, CA 94538
  Web site: http://startwithastory.wordpress.com/

COLORADO

Colorado Family Education, Resources & Training (CFERT)
  Telephone: 800 457-2736; 970-491-3904
  Address: 700 S., Mason Institute of Applied Prevention Research
    (Sage Hall), Fort Collins, CO
  E-mail: cweitzel@colotate.edu
  Web site: www.ext.colostate.edu
  Contact: Christine Cerbana, CFERT Program Director; *e-mail:*
    christine.cerbana@colostate.edu; *direct phone:* 970-491-2101

CONNECTICUT

Families in Crisis, Inc
  Telephone: 860-727 5800
  Address: 60 Popieluszko Court, Hartford, CT 06106.
  E-mail: www.familiesincrisis.org
  Web site: www.familiesincrisis.org

Fresh Start Community Reentry Program
  Telephone: 203-838-0496
  Address: Administrative Offices, 9 Mott Avenue, Suite 104,
    Norwalk, CT 06850
  E-mail: info@familyreentry.org
  Web site: www.familyreentry.org

GEORGIA

Foreverfamily
Telephone: 404-658-9606
Address: 765 McDaniel Street, S.W., Suite 3104, Atlanta, GA 30310
Web site: http://www.foreverfam.org/

Camp Hope, Mentors4Hope, Interns4Tomorrow
Telephone: 770-977-7751
Address: 4385 Lower Roswell Road, Marietta, GA 30068
E-mail: info@kidz2leaders.org
Web site: www.kidz2leaders.org

HAWAII

Supporting Families Affected by Incarceration.
Telephone: 808-843-2502
Address: 3097 Kalihi Street, Honolulu, HI 96819
E-mail: contact@keikiokaain.org
Web site: www.keikiokaaina.org

ILLINOIS

Women of Power Alumni Association
Telephone: 773-674-7731
Address: 2801 S. Rockwell Avenue, Chicago, IL 60608
E-mail: swjp@cookcountysheriff.org.
Web site: www.cookcountysheriff.org

INDIANA

Ties That Bind Us
Telephone: 217-241-9911
Address: 1209 S. 4th Street, Springfield, IL 62704
Web site: www.towerofrefugeinc.com

KANSAS

Arts in Prison, Inc
Telephone: 913-403-0229
Address: 1333 S. 27th Street, Kansas City, KS 66106

E-mail: info@artsinprison.org
Web site: www.artsinprison.org

LOUISIANA

Someone to Watch Over Me
  Telephone: 504-908-6277
  Address: 4000 Magazine Street, New Orleans, LA 70115
  E-mail: cscnouw@aol.com
  Web site: www.cscnouw.org

MARYLAND

Project SIT
  Telephone: 410-548-4850, Ext. 361
  Address: 411 Naylor Mill Road, Salisbury, MD 21801
  E-mail: sit@wicomicocounty.org

MASSACHUSETTS

CAI Head Start
  Telephone: 978-372-5052
  Address: 75 Elm Street, Haverhill, MA 03104
  E-mail: dlinett@communityactioninc.org
  Web site: www.communityactioninc.org

MINNESOTA

Family Strengthening Project
  Telephone: 612-353-3000
  Address: 822 South Third Street, Suite 100, Minneapolis, MN 55415
  E-mail: info@crimeandjustice.org
  Web site: www.crimeandjustice.org

Kinship of Greater Minneapoli
  Telephone: 612-588-4655
  Address: 3210 Oliver Ave. N, Minneapolis, MN 55412
  E-mail: mail@kinship.org
  Web site: www.kinship.org

MISSISSIPPI

The Storybook Project
    Telephone: 601-352-7125
    Address: P.O. Box 23815, Jackson, MS
    E-mail: csullivan@lesm.org
    Web site: www.lesm.org

MISSOURI

Let's Start
    Telephone: 314-241-2324.
    Address: 1408 S. 10th Street, St. Louis MO 63104
    Web site: www.letsstart.org

ParentLink
    Telephone: 800-552-8522
    Address: 4800 Santana Circle, Columbia, MO 65211
    E-mail: parentlink@missouri.edu
    Web site: http://parentlink.missouri.edu

University of Missouri Extension 4-H LIFE Program
    Telephone: 573-882-3316
    Address: 828 Clark Hall, Columbia, MO 65211
    E-mail: gillespiet@missouri.edu
    Web site: extension.missouri.edu/4hlife

MONTANA

Montana Alliance for Families Touched by Incarceration (MAFTI)
    Telephone: 406-728-5437
    Address: 1644 S. 8th, West Missoula, MT 59825
    E-mail: marty@parentingplace.net

NEBRASKA

Parenting Program
    Telephone: 402-362-3317
    Address: 1107 Recharge Road, York, NE 68467
    E-mail: mary.alley@nebraska.gov

NEW HAMPSHIRE

Family Connections Center
   Telephone: 603-271-2255
   Address: PO Box 14, Concord, NH 03237
   E-mail: FccConcord@nhdoc.state.nh.us
   Web site: www.nh.gov/nhdoc/fcc.

NEW MEXICO

Parent Reentry Programming
   Telephone: 505-877-7060
   Address: 1101 Lopez Road SW, Albuquerque, NM 87105
   E-mail: info@pbjfamilyservices.org
   Web site: www.pbjfamilyservices.org

NEW YORK

Fathers Count/Re-Entry Plus
   Telephone: 914-937-2320
   Address: One Gateway Plaza, 4th floor, Port Chester, NY 10573
   Web site: www.fsw.org

Prison Families Anonymous
   Telephone: 631-943-0441
   Address: Sarisohn Law Building, 350 Veterans Highway (RT 454),
      Commack, NY 11725
   E-mail: pfa.longisland@gmail.com
   Web site: www.pfa-li.com

The Fortune Society
   Telephone: 212-691-7554
   Address: 29-76 Northern Boulevard, Long Island City, NY 11101
   E-mail: http://fortunesociety.org/

The Gang Diversion, Reentry and Absent
Fathers Intervention Centers, Inc.
   Telephone: 718-694-8357
   Address: 116 Nassau Street, 7th floor, Brooklyn, NY 11201.

Long Island Council on Alcoholism and Drug Dependence
   Telephone: 516-747-2606

Address: 207 Hillside Avenue, Williston Park, NY

E-mail: recover@licadd.org

Web site: www.licadd.org

Osborne Association

Telephone: 718-707-2684

Address: 809 Westchester Avenue, Bronx, NY 10455

E-mail: kimora@osborneny.org

Web site: www.osborneny.org

NORTH CAROLINA

Harriet's House

Telephone: 919-834-0666, ext. 235

Address: P.O. Box 10347, 712 West Johnson Street, Raleigh, NC 27605

E-mail: www.passagehome.org

Web site: www.passagehome.org

Offender Family Services

Telephone: 919-838-3629

Address: 840 W. Morgan Street, 4280 MSC, Raleigh, NC

E-mail: wmn01@doc.state.nc.us

Web site: www.doc.state.nc.us/familyservices/

Our Children's Place

Telephone: 919-843-2670

Address: P.O. Box 1086, Chapel Hill, NC 27514

E-mail: ourchildrensplace@gmail.com

Web site: www.ourchildrensplace.com

OHIO

Butler County Reentry Initiative

Telephone: 513-424-8284

Address: 1105 Fourteenth Avenue, Middletown, OH 45044

E-mail: 3rdevelopment@sbcglobal.net

OKLAHOMA

Passport to the Future.
>*Telephone:* 580-298-2921
>*Address:* 603 S.W. "B" Street, Antlers, OK 74523
>*E-mail:* dlong@littledixie.org
>*Web site:* www.littledixie.org

PENNSYLVANIA

Families Outside
>*Telephone:* 412-820-2050
>*Address:* 3230 William Pitt Way, Pittsburgh, PA 15238
>*E-mail:* fswp@fswp.org
>*Web site:* www.fswp.org

Girl Scouts beyond Bars
>*Telephone:* 888-564-2030
>*Address:* P.O. Box 27540, Philadelphia, PA 19118
>*E-mail:* info@gsep.org

Youth Support Program
>*Telephone:* 717-299-2831
>*Address:* 630 Janet Avenue, Lancaster, PA 17601
>*E-mail:* info@compassmark.org
>*Web site:* www.compassmark.org

RHODE ISLAND

Rhode Islanders Sponsoring Education (RISE)
>*Telephone:* 401-421-2010
>*Address:* 17 Gordon Avenue, Suite 004, Providence, RI 02905
>*E-mail:* santaya@riseonline.org
>*Web site:* www.riseonline.org

SOUTH CAROLINA

Department of Young Offender Services
>*Telephone:* 803-896-1774
>*Address:* 4444 Broad River Road, Columbia, SC 29210

E-mail: doc.state.sc.us
Web site: www.doc.sc.gov/programs/yoprs.jsp

TENNESSEE

Ties That Bind Us
   Address: 1380 Poplar Avenue, Memphis, TN 38125
   E-mail: info@familiesofncarcerated.org
   Web site: www.familiesofincarcerated.org

TEXAS

National Prisoner's Family Conference
   Telephone: 915-861-7733
   Address: 2200 N. Yarbrough, B 245, El Paso, TX 79925
   E-mail: info@prisonersfamilyconference.org
   Web site: www.prisonersfamilyconference.org

Against the Odds (ATO) Mentoring Program
   Telephone: 214-421-1373
   Address: 2610 Martin Luther King Jr. Boulevard, Dallas, TX 75215
   E-mail: atomentoring@sbcglobal.net
   Web site: www.southfaircdc.org

Counseling and Assessment Preparation Center (CAP)
   Telephone: 956-381-5251
   Address: 1201 W. University Drive, EDCC 1.272, Edinburg, TX 78539
   E-mail: syalafa@utpa.edu

DePelchin Children's Center
   Telephone: 713-730-2335
   Address: 4950 Memorial Drive, Houston, TX 77007
   E-mail: info@depelchin.org
   Web site: www.depelchin.org

Seedling's Promise
   Telephone: 512-323-6371
   Address: 2800 S., IH 35, Suite 170, Austin, TX 78704
   E-mail: info@seedlingfoundation.org
   Web site: seedlingfoundation.org

VERMONT

Community H.S. of Vermont
    Telephone: 802-951-5037
    Address: 103 South Main Street, Waterbury, VT 05671-1001
    E-mail: charity.baker@state.vt.us
    Web site: www.doc.state.vt.us/programs/educational-programs/

Kids-A-Part
    Telephone: 802-859-3227
    Address: 79 Weaver St, P.O. Box 127, Winooski, VT 05404
    E-mail: mainadmn@vtcas.org
    Web site: www.lundvt.org/kids-apart.html

VIRGINIA

Resource Information Help for the Disadvantaged
    Telephone: 804-426-4426
    Address: RIHD c/o WMUMC, 1720 Mechanicsville Turnpike,
        Richmond, VA 23223
    E-mail: InMateResource@yahoo.com
    Web site: www.rihd.org

The Messages Project
    Address: P.O. Box 8325, Norfolk, VA 23503
    E-mail: list@themessagesproject.org
    Web site: http://www.themessagesproject.org/

ACKNOWLEDGMENTS

We wish to thank Barbara Allan, founder and director of Prison Families Anonymous, who for forty years has been dedicated to making sure that the silenced voices of prison families be heard, in a widespread effort to change policies and attitudes affecting every aspect of their lives. Despite the many demands on Barbara's schedule—local, national, and international—she has made sure to join our high school writers almost every Wednesday afternoon, becoming their first audience as they created new chapters and scenes, providing support and resources for them while letting them know that their stories will be taken into the world. She has taken in these young people as fellow writers, as she finishes her own book, *Doing Time on the Outside,* in their workshop.

We wish to thank Rachel Wiener, director of the Center for Peace at Central Islip High School, for her role as mother and mentor to the group. Without Rachel's careful selection of each student participant and encouragement throughout, whenever things got hard, our project never would have come to fruition. Both Rachel and Barbara were able to build on what came out of the writing to offer support in a myriad of other aspects of the students' lives.

We thank Rob Goldman, of Tikkun Long Island, an organization dedicated to restorative justice, for bringing the project to the attention of Touro Law Center, linking storytelling and the law in a way that will forever after guide us, and for providing both financial support for the project and a cadre of volunteers who wrote along with the students.

We thank Thomas Maligno, director of Touro Law Center's Public Advocacy Center, for creating a structure in which law students could participate in the project as part of their pro bono requirement, creating a format in which law interns could learn about the real-life issues affecting those they would someday serve, while the high school students could be inspired to consider careers in policy making and law. We thank the Public Advocacy Center for providing space for our meetings.

We thank New York State Assemblyman Phil Ramos for hosting our student readers each year in performances for government officials, educators and human service providers, and for inviting the young people to present their stories for the state legislature in Albany. His openness to their stories and pride in having them among his constituents has contributed greatly to their feeling that their writings matter.

We thank Kathleen Masterson of the Arts Education Program of New York State Council on the Arts (NYSCA), not only for major support of this program over the years, but for seeing the importance of a writing pedagogy based on the understanding of empathy in the area of community-based learning. We thank the National Endowment for the Arts (NEA), RTS Family Foundation, the Angela and Scott Jaggar Foundation and the Horace and Amy Hagedorn Fund for supplementary support. We thank Sol Marie Alfonso-Jones of Long Island Community Foundation for supporting Herstory's youth justice initiatives, where storytellers and activists join hands. We thank Jennifer Marino Rojas of the Rauch Foundation for helping us take this work to the next level.

We thank Alan Gold for the design of Herstory's folio editions and larger anthologies, memoirs, and teaching manuals that were used in the project, and Jim Harris, of G&H Soho, for his dedicated book printing support.

We thank Angela Zimmerman of Family Support Long Island at Molloy College, for bringing us together with Prison Families Anonymous to design an intentional way to raise the voices of the children of the incarcerated in the interest of healing, empowerment and change.

We thank the Knapp Swezey Foundation for providing the funding for Herstory's Patchogue Bridges to Justice community-based workshop, where the adult writers represented in this collection had the opportunity to work on book-length projects. In this workshop, Shanequa Levin, director of Every Child Matters on Long Island and president of Long Island Mocha Moms, began her coming-of-age story that celebrates the potential of every child to come to the full realization of her possibilities. There, she is bringing this book to completion. There, Amanda Acevedo, who just graduated from Stony Brook University's School of Social Welfare, uses her writing of her own story of growing up with a father in prison to guide her work with adolescents in Riverhead Correctional Facility, as she works with Herstory to learn how to lead writing workshops for incarcerated women and girls. There, Barbara Allan, founder of Prison Families Anonymous, began her own book before she switched to working with the high school writers as her first audience. We thank the Patchogue Arts Council for providing the space for this workshop each week.

Finally, we thank Cheryl Hamilton, director of Stony Brook University's Educational Opportunity Program for including Herstory programming in their summer institute for students transitioning from high school to college, out of which Katherine De la Cruz's powerful story, reprinted in this volume, was born.

We thank the ten writers in this collection, for giving not only their words, but their whole hearts to this journey, and for giving so much back to the world.

Erika Duncan, Founder and Co-Director
Herstory Writers Workshop
Editor for this collection

Serena Liguori, Co-Director
Hersory Writers Workshop

NOTES

NOTES